Adolphe Fourier de Bacourt

Souvenirs of a Diplomat

Private letters from America during the Administration of Presidents Van Buren,

Harrison, and Tyler

Adolphe Fourier de Bacourt

Souvenirs of a Diplomat

Private letters from America during the Administration of Presidents Van Buren, Harrison, and Tyler

ISBN/EAN: 9783744715768

Printed in Europe, USA, Canada, Australia, Japan

Cover: Foto ©ninafisch / pixelio.de

More available books at **www.hansebooks.com**

SOUVENIRS OF A DIPLOMAT

*Private Letters from America during the Administrations of
Presidents VAN BUREN, HARRISON, and TYLER*

BY

THE CHEVALIER DE BACOURT

Minister from France

WITH A MEMOIR OF THE AUTHOR

BY THE COMTESSE DE MIRABEAU

Translated from the French

NEW YORK
HENRY HOLT AND COMPANY
1885

M. DE BACOURT.

I FOUND these letters on America amongst the papers of my uncle, M. de Bacourt.

When he was Minister-Plenipotentiary at Washington every packet-boat leaving for France brought accounts and criticisms of what he saw and heard day by day. Later, these letters, preserved with care, were returned to him. They describe the United States so well, such as it was forty years ago, that I have thought it my duty to publish them.

What struck me particularly in copying them was, that a republican form of government was far from offering a satisfactory result, even in that country, which had never to contend against any remembrance of monarchy, or against any party or opposition. This nation, newly born, free from all oppression and servitude, rich and independent, seemed gloomy and discontented, inspiring one with painful feelings. While following with curiosity these people, who are forming and organizing themselves, one feels ill at ease in this vast and beautiful country, where the only passions—very contradictory ones—are the love of money and the love of liberty.

There is nothing to sympathize with, nothing to inspire confidence, nothing to admire. One sees the representatives of the nation insulting each other and fighting with fists and knives in the streets and other public places—even in the halls of Congress; the Minister of Foreign Affairs gets drunk at a dinner given by the President of the United States to the Diplomatic Corps. Their manners are entirely without refinement, and with no rules to govern them.

I think it right to mention here the personal history of the writer of these letters, whose memory is by a singular chance connected with two great historic characters—" Mirabeau and Talleyrand."

Born in 1801, he entered diplomatic life in 1822. He was Ambassador at Turin when he sent, the day before the revolution of February, his resignation to M. de Lamartine. He did not ally himself to any government. Some he thought too near anarchy, and others too despotic. His early retirement was for him a great sacrifice, for he took a deep and constant interest in public affairs; but he would not trifle either with his convictions or with his political beliefs.

At the commencement of his career he had known at the Hague the Count de la Marck, Prince of Arenberg, to whom Mirabeau wrote on July 17, 1790:

"Here, my dear Count, are two packets, that you will give up only to me whatever happens, and in case of my death you will confide to one who will take enough interest in my memory to defend it."

The Count de la Marck replied:

"The most anxious desire to serve you will teach me to choose those who will be most worthy to serve you."

Forty years later he confided the defence "of the great tribune" to M. de Bacourt, who during his active and wandering career could not attend to it, and it was not until 1851 that the "Correspondence of Mirabeau" appeared; in 1848 I had married the grand-nephew of Mirabeau, without my uncle, who always treated me as an adopted daughter, having in any way aided this marriage; but this singular coincidence caused him to take more to heart the commission confided to him.

The "Correspondence of Mirabeau" established clearly and precisely his sentiments and convictions. This man, who had committed only faults and was treated as a criminal, had dearly bought the right to combat those arbitrary laws of which he was the victim. He wished to put some bounds to the power without limit and without control which had caused him to pass the greater part of his life in the States' prison. Later, it is true, he tried to modify the Revolution and to establish the government on a constitutional basis, but he did not sell himself as he was accused of doing, since in trying to save the expiring monarchy he only obeyed his own convictions. He had made '89, but would have nothing to do with '93.

Pursued by his creditors, obliged to write day by day books and pamphlets to obtain money to satisfy their demands, forced to fly from them, miserably shackled, he had neither liberty of mind nor time; and it was under these circumstances and to enter in full possession of his genius that he accepted from the court the payment of his debts.

In allowing himself to be relieved of the chains which weighed on his life he most certainly thought neither of making his fortune nor even of setting a price on his eloquence; and a letter addressed to Mademoiselle de Nehra proves conclusively his indifference to his personal interests, for in the midst of the most cruel pecuniary difficulties he answers his mistress who asks him about one of his lawsuits:

"I have other things to do than to think of all these trifles. Do you know the situation we are in? Do you know that speculation is at its height? Do you know that soon there will be not one cent in the public treasury?"

And when he wrote that, his own purse did not contain a farthing! This cry of distress is the unanswerable proof that Mirabeau had a passionate love for his country and a thorough contempt for money.

Immediately after the publication of the letters of Mirabeau, M. de Bacourt was busy with the memoirs of Talleyrand. He had been sent in 1830 on a mission to the illustrious diplomat, who then represented France in England. Scarcely had M. de Talleyrand seen him than he asked to be allowed to keep him, and immediately promoted him to the rank of first secretary of the embassy. The prince had still great skill in affairs, a quickness of judgment, and that persevering will before which so many powers had yielded, but his age would not allow him to give much time to work. His young secretary, who could understand his views from a single word, became a necessary adjunct. Many chiefs would not have been willing to acknowledge this, but M. de Talleyrand said so openly to King Louis-Philippe in recommending my uncle to him, and during an absence of four months that he was obliged to make on account of his health, he intrusted to this diplomat, then only twenty-eight years of age, the absolute direction of affairs which were being treated at London, and which at this time were the most important in Europe.

Some years later, when the Prince, who had been for a long time in retirement at Paris, felt his end drawing near, he called to him M. de Bacourt, who shared with his family the care of reconciling him to the Church: every one worked with heart and soul to accomplish this object, and he who had for half a century led Europe, threw, for perhaps the first time, a look beyond the boundaries of this world; at this moment, a child beautiful as the day, clothed in white and covered with a long veil, knelt at his feet and asked his blessing. It was the daughter of Baron Talleyrand,— Madame Stanley,—who was going to make her first communion. The Bishop of Autun, profoundly moved, blessed her. In a few minutes he was converted!

Although his love for dynastic government had fallen off, M. de Talleyrand strove always and above everything to keep or to give to his country its force and its splendor. He knew under all circumstances how to serve France usefully and powerfully, and when she was invaded by Europe, it was a wonderful success on his part, at the Congress of Vienna, to have retained her frontiers intact. This great and clever diplomat deserved truly to be called "The Liberator of the Country."

By his will, dated January 10, 1834, M. de Talleyrand had appointed his niece the Duchess de Dino residuary legatee and executrix of his will, enjoining her in the most formal manner not to publish his memoirs until thirty years after his death. By two codicils, dated May 13, 1837, and March 17, 1838, the Prince appointed M. de Bacourt to replace the Duchess de Dino in case she had not survived after the delay of thirty years, and he bequeathed to his two executors the right to postpone the publication of the memoirs if they judged it necessary.

M. de Talleyrand died May 18, 1838, and the Duchess de Dino, become Duchess Talleyrand and Sagan, September 19, 1862; but a long time before her death she had placed in my uncle's hands all the Prince's papers.

It was considerable work to arrange in their proper order the different parts of these memoirs, for M. de Talleyrand, whenever an important event occurred, put it in writing and tossed it amongst other notes.

M. de Bacourt wishing to support these

memoirs of the Prince by authentic documents, travelled through Europe many times for the purpose of searching the archives in the legations for proofs not necessary for his own satisfaction, but for history, and, having a presentiment that his end was near, he worked during the latter part of his life as much as ten hours a day that he might not leave his task unfinished.

My mother, residuary legatee and executrix of my uncle's will, was charged by him to place the *Memoirs* of Prince Talleyrand with Messrs. Châtelain and Paul Andral, who have had them now seventeen years. The article in the will of my uncle relating to this trust ends thus: "I impose as an express condition on Messrs. Châtelain and Andral that no publication shall be made of these papers before the year 1888;" thus adding a term of twenty years to the thirty fixed by Prince Talleyrand.

A sum of ten thousand francs was also bequeathed by M. de Bacourt to Messrs. Châtelain and Andral to indemnify them for keeping and publishing the memoirs of M. de Talleyrand.

It is evident from this explanation that the

holders of these memoirs have not the right to publish a single line before the year 1888, and consequently the rumors announcing their publication before that time can have no foundation.

It is not for me to explain at this day the motives which induced my uncle to impose this long delay, but it is certain that in doing so he sacrificed his own interests, for the publication made during his life or soon after his death would have attached a great importance to his name.

During the years he passed in retirement, as I have said, he was busy with these various works, which obliged him to make many and long journeys; besides which, his friendship with illustrious persons often called him abroad.

From 1835 to 1840 he had been Minister of France to Carlsruhe; the Grand Duke was very much attached to him, and he was also particularly well received by the Grand Duchess Dowager Stephanie, aunt of Napoleon III., who at that time was obliged to remain in Carlsruhe under the surveillance of the Minister of France, and from time to time to show herself at the Legation. No one foresaw at that time that the Prince who lived in this painful dependence would one day ascend the throne that he had endeavored to destroy by his conspiracies, which were called by every one "acts of a madman." The boat which carried "Cæsar and his fortunes" seemed then a long way from shore.

While still retaining his relations with the Court of Baden, M. de Bacourt went often to visit the Grand Duchess Stephanie at Coblentz, and was there when her grand daughter, the Princess Caroline Wasa, refused to become the Empress of the French. It was nevertheless the dream of the Grand Duchess, and the earnest wish of Napoleon III., who had an interview with the little Princess at Baden; but she thought her cousin "too old"!

She was then eighteen years of age and the Emperor forty-four. Then, she, descended from the kings of Sweden, who were dispossessed by Napoleon I., would not marry a Bonaparte. An Imperial throne seemed nevertheless a great position for an exiled princess; but not allowing herself to be dazzled or influenced, she resisted all entreaties with great energy.

One year after, she married the Prince of Saxony, and is at this day queen of that little kingdom.

The Grand-duchess Stephanie had in 1849 presented M. de Bacourt to the Prince and Princess of Prussia, who lived in the château de Coblentz a great part of the year. He, who was to become later a very powerful monarch, lived at this time removed from politics, often indeed from the court, and so long as his brother could reign, contented himself with being the first subject of the king. My uncle, admitted during fifteen years to the intimacy of the Emperor of Germany, saw a great deal of the Prince Hereditary, and his charming sister, the Duchess of Baden; he had a deep attachment for the House of Prussia, and if anything could console us for his premature loss, it would be to think that the pain of witnessing the war of 1870 had been spared him.

I hope that these letters on America may recall the remembrance of M. de Bacourt to his friends: he wrote them without a thought of their ever being published. In re-writing them I seem to hear him talk and to see him again amongst us; for every page shows the natural originality which made the most trifling anecdote amusing. His intellect was of a superior order; he had the gift of repartee, a great facility for work, a sound judgment from which nothing could move him, and a penetration quick and sure which in the diplomatic career assures success: these qualities enabled him to foresee events both in things concerning his private life and in political questions relating to France and foreign countries. It is to be remarked in this correspondence from 1840 to 1842 that he foresaw fifteen years beforehand the bloody drama that would divide the North and the South into two fields, where their hatreds and rivalries would cause them to forget the common interests of their country.

Of an agreeable appearance in his youth, he always retained an exceptional elegance; distinguished, simple, and natural, he not only knew how to please, but he knew also how to make himself loved; while keeping himself in the background with extreme reserve, he never passed unobserved, and before being "something" he was "some one."

He had the talent of raising himself without

exciting any feeling of enmity: this has often been said to his credit. He was generous and devoted, but never gave his support to any one who did not merit his esteem. Above all, he was honest and firm; and Prince Talleyrand wrote to King Louis-Philippe, "I know few people whose mind can be compared to that of M. de Bacourt, and I never have known any one more honest."

One word only, strikingly just, said pleasantly by him, would often take the place of advice, and better attain the end sought. Here, where I write these lines, about thirty-five years ago I entered his room by climbing a window of the ground-floor, and said to him, probably with a pert manner, "Will you come and walk with me, uncle?" He replied, "Willingly, nephew."

He always had a great affection for my mother, and my father before becoming his brother-in-law was his most intimate and respected friend. We lived together when he was not abroad, and I could appreciate during all my life the great value of his character, his intelligence, and his heart. Something would be wanting to this portrait if I neglected to say that his beliefs were always firm, and his death admirably Christian.

I feel sure that no one who has known him will think these eulogies exaggerated: they have been inspired by his memory, and the filial love I have always had for him.

COUNTESS MIRABEAU.

COSSESSEVILLE, June 1, 1882.

SOUVENIRS OF A DIPLOMAT.

I.

LONDON, May 24, 1840.

I HAVE been to see M. Guizot. I found this little ambassador comfortably installed in his magnificent house, content with his position, with the progress of affairs, with all the world, with everything, but complaining of a feeling of loneliness in this great turmoil of London. I hear that he has some success as a wit, but that no one cares to be intimate with him. He goes most frequently to Holland House and to Mrs. Stanley's, wife of Edward Stanley, who is somewhat of a radical. It was thought in very bad taste on his part that he should have asked Mrs. Stanley to invite O'Connell to meet him at dinner.

London is much more lively than it was five years ago. The shops are more brilliant;

there is a luxurious display, a magnificence, which throw in the shade all that Paris can offer, though the *luxe* there is very great! . . . I should be tempted to believe with M. Guizot that a country where every kind of industry is developed to such a degree is in no danger of a revolution, if other signs did not excite my uneasiness. It is like in France, where a bad crop will compromise the existence of a Government.

Besides, here there is an ill-feeling towards the Queen, the Government is without moral force, the Ministry in a minority in Parliament at least once a month; radicalism makes slow but sure progress, and the aristocracy loses every day some of its influence in favor of the middle class, which is ambitious and agitated. England is also somewhat seriously embarrassed in her relations with Portugal, Spain, Naples, Egypt, Greece, and the United States.

Her foreign policy is directed by a man who has ability, but vacillating, always throwing himself into new difficulties before getting out of those brought on by his own imprudent levity. His colleagues feel this, know it, but to remedy it one of them would have to take the direction of foreign affairs, and they are either too indolent or too incapable to do so. Now you have my idea of the state of this country since my arrival; I bound myself to give you my impressions, false or true, at the risk of having to retract if anything should alter them later.

I dined with Lady Burghersh at the house of the poor little Countess Bathyani. The talk was almost entirely of the small scandals of London society, and particularly of Lady Jersey. Lord William Russell, her brother-in-law, had just been murdered; this caused her to deplore very much, a few days ago, in the presence of the Duchess of Gloucester, the necessity she was under of putting off her mourning to go to the Drawing-room. The good Duchess of Gloucester told this to the Queen, who charged her aunt to say to Lady Jersey that she could understand her embarrassment, and would dispense with her presence at the Drawing-room. Lady Jersey, furious at not being able to go to Court, tried to persuade the Duchess of Gloucester, who perceived too late that she had been made a dupe of, that notwithstanding the permission of the Queen, she owed it to her daughter, the Countess Sarah, to take her to the Drawing-room. They say it was a very funny scene, and she was obliged, to her great regret, to give it up.

II.

May 26, 1840.

I HAVE seen Lord Grey; he is very bitter about the prospect of affairs, and not at all happy in growing old. I returned to M. Guizot's: he has great assurance, and directs affairs with a high hand. He showed me a letter of twelve pages from M. Thiers, but did not read it to me. It crossed my mind that there was probably an understanding between these two to deceive *him*, who ought to be their master. M. Guizot is very polite to me; complimented me very much on the impression I had left in London, but he asked me so often when I proposed leaving that I was inclined to think that my presence annoyed him. I am to dine with him to-day.

III.

May 24, 1840.

THE dinner at the French Embassy, after the fashion of Louis Esbrat, was very good, the appointments of the table elegant enough, but as unlike that of the time of M. de Talleyrand as the two men were. M. Guizot did his best to make the conversation lively, praised his wine with the air of a connoisseur while drinking and passing it round; but all that is studied, *and is not genuine.**

IV.

May 28, 1840.

I HAVE been to see Lady Palmerston, who looks much younger and is much gayer. She spoke to me of her uneasiness at the arrival of Madame de Lieven; she said that Bulow was so agitated about it that it made him nervous and sick. Lord Palmerston, with whom I passed two hours, has been frank and precise

---

* All English words in italics throughout the book are generally M. de Bacourt's own—or his printers', and sometimes justify careful observation.

in his explanation of the position of affairs in America and Buenos Ayres that I had to treat of with him; he has accepted my assistance in America, and says he will send me a letter for Mr. Fox, English Minister at Washington, in which he will speak of me in such a manner as to establish the best relations between us. He has clearly explained to me, and I think honestly, the cause of the coolness existing for the last two years between France and England. I am perfectly satisfied with this interview, the results of which will be very useful to me on the other side of the Atlantic. I have dined with Mr. Ellis, who has a real affection for Thiers; he says that Thiers and Guizot understand each other like two fingers on the same hand.

V.

LONDON, May 29, 1840.

I THOUGHT it my duty to give M. Guizot an account of my conversation with Lord Palmerston. He began the conversation by inquiring when I proposed leaving. He cannot conceal the pleasure he feels in the rejection by the Chamber of Deputies of the bill appropriating a million for the erection of a statue of Napoleon: he sees in that a defeat for the Ministry, and rejoices in it. Altogether, he was more free and unreserved in his conversation. He said that M. Thiers, with his nature, could never resist the Left, and would be drawn in by them. It is a bad moment to pass; the troubled waters must flow off. He accepted congratulations on the inheritance which must come to him on the fall of his friend, with whom "he is like two fingers on the same hand." He expects the Princess de Lieven on the 15th of June, and shows no uneasiness about her coming; he pretends to be astonished at the terror of De Brunow and De Bulow, whom he laughs at; in fine, he hopes to settle the affairs of the East, and after this triumph to return to France and " mount the Capitol."

VI.

CLIFTON, NEAR BRISTOL, June 3, 1840.

I LEFT London yesterday. I am well cured of my admiration for the public carriages of England—only fit to carry travelling agents of robust health, and pressed for time. From London to Bath we passed through a beautiful country, justly called the garden of England. I am here in a small inn on the banks of the Avon, at a hundred yards' distance from the bay where the Great Western lies: they proposed giving me an apartment overlooking the bay; I refused. I shall see soon enough the ship which carries me over there.

VII.

Globe Hotel, New York, June 19, 1840.

I FOUND no pleasure in the voyage, and I fear that you will not find much in reading the narrative which I now resume from the time of my departure. Before quitting England I wished to see the country around Clifton, so celebrated for its picturesque sites. The little river Avon after leaving Bristol enters a gorge seven miles in length, each bank formed by perpendicular rocks. They are now building a suspension bridge as strong as that of Fribourg across the river, and while waiting its completion the passage is made through the air in baskets sliding on chains.

We went on board on June 4, at the mouth of the Avon, where the Great Western was anchored. General Chatry de la Fosse cried bitterly at parting with his son, whom he had accompanied here. The Great Western is a magnificent boat of two hundred and twenty-six feet in length, by fifty-four in breadth and forty-nine feet deep. The steam-engine is of four hundred and fifty horse-power. It is imposing to look at from far off or near by. Now, if you will allow me, we will examine the interior, and you can judge if it is as agreeable to live in. The deck is divided into three parts: forward, occupied by the crew, servants, etc. etc.; the middle, where the engine is, and what I call the menagerie; and the after part, where the passengers have a large space to walk in. Upon the after-deck there is a large saloon, the centre of which is glazed to give light to the dining-room which is below; around these two are the passengers' cabins. The engine and the menagerie occupy the centre. The cabins of the domestics, those of the crew, and the kitchens occupy the part below the forward deck. All this is well arranged, grand to see; but God help the nervous invalids who live there. In this space that I have described are packed together eighty-five passengers, men, women, and children; ninety-two of the crew, twenty-five of whom are negroes or mulattoes, justly celebrated for their disagreeable odor; then there are two cows, twelve pigs, ten sheep, twenty-five chickens, and as many ducks, geese, and turkeys, not one of which was killed on the voyage, being reserved for the return passage. Imagine all these drinking, eating, sleeping, crying, singing, bellowing, bleating, add to this the noise of the engine and the orders for the management of the vessel; imagine yourself shut up in a state-room seven feet long, seven feet wide, and seven feet high,—and you will have a correct idea of the pleasure of the voyage. It is nothing when the weather is good and the sea calm; but if the sea is rough, half of these people are sick, so are the animals; then it becomes an infernal abode.

We weighed anchor the 4th of June at four o'clock in the afternoon, and proceeded down the Bristol Channel, bounded on one side by the coast of Ireland, and on the other by the high rocky shores of Devonshire and Cornwall, covered with verdure. Leaving the Bristol Channel we encountered a north-west wind, which was against us, and continued until last night, making our voyage much rougher; but the Great Western—which, we may truly say, makes her way in spite of wind or wave—stopped for nothing; on the fourteenth day we entered the port of New York.

On the 10th the sea rose very high and the

night was terrible, but at all events I had the pleasure of seeing a real tempest. On the 13th we met a French fishing-boat of Saint-Malo, which had been out four months. The meeting of any vessel is a great event, being a quarter of an hour's distraction from the most killing monotony. On the 15th a cry of alarm was heard, and the engine stopped suddenly; a general panic took possession of every one; they tumbled out of their berths; some cried fire, and others that the boiler was going to burst. The agony was great. The fact was that a poor sailor while fixing something in the rigging had fallen overboard; the whole length of the vessel had passed over him without touching him — a real miracle! They threw a boat into the sea, and as he was a good swimmer he was soon fished out. The whole affair only lasted fifteen minutes, thanks to the admirable English discipline. We took an American pilot on the 18th, and that night about one o'clock we entered the port of New York, and went on shore at five o'clock in the morning.

VIII.

New York, June 20, 1840.

I FOUND it delightful to sleep in a bed after fifteen nights' confinement in a kind of coffin. I have come to the conclusion, after the voyage I have made: in the first place, that I am a very bad sailor; and in the second, that the sea is a very sad element, and that life at sea is perfectly insipid. The imagination of poets may find in the immensity of water and sky beauties that I have never seen, but I declare to you that the rising and setting of the sun, the moon, and the stars are just as beautiful on land as at sea.

Yesterday I went on shore with M. de la Fosse, with whom, I will say here, I was much pleased during the passage. We went immediately to the office of the Consul-General, M. de la Forest; he was absent, and we were obliged to seek the Vice-Consul, a little fool, who so badly managed affairs that we could not get our luggage until late in the afternoon. I shall pass a week here probably to settle some business matters. I have seen nothing of the city yet, except in going and coming from the consulate to the hotel. The first impression is not favorable: the houses are ugly, built of brick, with areas in the English fashion; stone sidewalks everywhere; and streets paved with large cobble-stones—very bad for carriages and disagreeable for those who ride in them; many of the streets are planted with trees; it has the appearance of a large provincial town, with a mixture of Dutch; and there is the constant busy movement of a mercantile population of three hundred thousand souls.

IX.

NEW YORK, June 21, 1840.

I HAVE not been able to quiet my spirits, and have a feeling of deep sadness and regret already for that other part of the world which seems to me the best. I have been to the Battery—the only thing I was curious to see, because of its association in my mind with M. de Talleyrand and his adventure with M. Beaumetz. It is an ancient fortification, which forms the southern point of a peninsula on which the city of New York is situated. This Battery is now occupied by an amphitheatre built of painted boards, in which are given sometimes equestrian and other performances, and at other times is used as a public café; it is in very bad taste, and disfigures an interesting place. From the platform on top the view is large: one of the shores of this peninsula is washed by the North River, also called the Hudson, and the other by the East River, which is really a branch of the sea coming out of the bay of Long Island; these two rivers flow into each other opposite the Battery and form the harbor of New York, which is interspersed with lovely islands covered with verdure, beyond which can be seen the inhabited shores of New Jersey covered with trees. Innumerable vessels of all kinds occupy the banks of the two rivers: that of the Hudson is reserved for boats which are navigated through the canals and rivers in the interior of the United States; that of the East receives vessels arriving from or leaving for all parts of the globe. These sailing-vessels and steamers of every size, going and coming in every direction, add greatly to the beauty of New York.

On descending from the Battery you enter a little *square*, the trees in which are withered by the winds from the sea. From this square commences the great street of New York, Broadway, which runs parallel with the two rivers, and at an equal distance from each, for the space of three miles; cross streets run to the banks of each river from Broadway, and it is in this way that the city is built, extending very far in this shape, and growing larger every day. In 1731 the population of this great commercial city was 8000; now it is 300,000. Broadway is the principal street; all the shops are there, the handsomest houses, and important establishments; but it has the air of a town sacrificed to trade: there is not a monument, or a well-built house, that is not spoiled by something narrow and of bad taste. With the exception of dirtily dressed negroes and negresses, all the men and women one meets are dressed in good taste, without any difference between the more or less rich. The men are of the English type, strong and robust, but not graceful. I have seen many women with red hair, but as yet have seen none of the much-talked-of American beauties.

X.

NEW YORK, June 22, 1840.

I HAVE already had a sample of the American climate: on my arrival the weather was cold, then suddenly changed to the most intense heat. I went to Mass yesterday in a church which had the appearance of a Protestant temple; it was crowded to suffocation—no doubt on account of the Fête-Dieu. The service was good, with the exception of the singing, the music being decidedly secular. Nobody visits here on Sunday, although New York is not as puritanical as Boston, where a few years ago they closed the streets with chains on Sundays and holydays to prevent carriages from passing. The number of strangers residing in New York have somewhat changed the manners and customs. If I can believe what M. Berger, a physician whom I saw this morning, told me, American puritanism cannot be worth much. He assured me that at the present time there were not four persons, even amongst those in the highest positions, who had not been bankrupt or on the point of being so, notwithstanding which they made no change in their habits of living acquired in prosperous times.

I have received a visit from one of my colleagues at Washington, M. de Nordin, chargé d'affaires of Sweden. He gives me a sad picture of Washington, where the Diplomatic Corps can find no resources but in their own circle, and whist is the only amusement they indulge in. M. de la Forest, the Consul, who has arrived from Philadelphia, has also been to see me: he is a quondam young man, stout, with an attempt at elegance; he has offered his services to me, and seems obliging. We shall see.

XI.

NEW YORK, June 23, 1840.

I HAVE been with M. de la Forest, talking over business matters with which I have been entrusted. The Consul is decidedly a good fellow, but just as he has been described to me—without brains. We have made a round of visits together. I have left with Messrs. Martinet and John Livingston letters from Bresson, who is a relation of theirs; they are men of distinction. I also took Baths' letters to Mr. Goodhue; he is one of the richest men in New York, and solid, which is exceptional. On leaving him I went to see Mr. James King, of the house of Prime, Ward & King, correspondents of the Hottinguers. Mr. James King has an older brother, Charles King, distinguished for his wit, whose acquaintance I also made. They are the sons of a Mr. King whom M. de Talleyrand knew very well, and who had been the friend of Washington, and Minister from America to London during the entire term of Washington's Presidency. Since the death of General Washington all the

Kings have been prominent in the opposition, which is called here the *Whig* Party,—that is to say, the aristocratic party,—who contend that the present form of government is too democratic, that it has corrupted the work of Washington and his friends, the founders of the Republic. The Messrs. King are among the leaders of this party, who are so violently opposed to the government. Every one agrees in acknowledging their personal merit. Mr. James King, who is the head of the house, has engaged me to dine with him the day after to-morrow, at his country-seat six miles from New York, and to bring M. de la Fosse with me.

I dined at my hotel with M. de la Fosse, and M. de la Forest took us in the evening to see M. and Madame F——: he says they are the only respectable French family residing in New York; it is with this family he passes all his time. The husband appeared to me very vulgar; the wife, who is better, and must have been pretty, is a grand-niece of M. de Sèze. They have five grown-up daughters, and two boys. The Consul says they are all very charming, and have only one fault—that of being poor. One of these young ladies sang remarkably; she had the same master who taught Madame Malibran, who made her *début* in New York. These ladies spoke of the powers of the Countess Merlin, who has made a great sensation here, particularly with her singing; and she has gone to Havana, but intends to pass next winter in the United States.

XII.

NEW YORK, June 26, 1840.

I DINED with M. de la Fosse the day before yesterday at the best restaurant in New York. We had a detestable dinner and very dear; and in the evening, for want of something to do, we went to *Niblo's Garden*, the Tivoli of this town, much lower than the *chaumière du Montparnasse*.

The country-seat of Mr. King is in New Jersey; in the park, which is quite large, and laid out in the English fashion, the potato generally takes the place of green turf: the American character must always show a little, even in his *luxe*. The house, built of a beautiful gray stone, is a square pavilion surrounded by a gallery supported by columns: at the end of the house are greenhouses, after the English fashion. The interior is also arranged and furnished in the English style. Everything is a weak imitation of the English. At present, America and the Americans give me the impression of an England and Englishmen of *second and third rate*—particularly those whose position is not so high as that of the family whom I dined with yesterday, who are considered the most aristocratic of the country.

The mistress of the house, who is forty years of age, is as faded as one of sixty would be in Europe; one can see, nevertheless, that she has been pretty. Mrs. Duer, her daughter, is fat and fresh; but her sister-in-law, Miss Duer, twenty years old, and very like Madame de Marescalchi, is entirely *passé*. Eighteen months ago she was the belle not only of New York, but of the United States. It seems that this is the case with all American women: generally very pretty from sixteen to eighteen, they soon lose their teeth, their color, and at twenty they look twice their age. The extreme changes in the climate are thought to be the cause. The other guests at dinner were Messrs. John and Charles King, brothers of the host; Mr. Duer, his son-in-law, and his father, a fine-looking man of seventy years of age; Mr. Astor, M. de la Forest, M. de la Fosse, and myself. All these gentlemen are well enough, no doubt, but are second-class English, notwithstanding they are amongst the *gentlemen* the most *refined* in this country. They try to be elegant, but you see that it is not their everyday manner, and that they feel embarrassed—with the exception of Mr. Duer, the father, who has the polish of olden times, with a distinguished appearance and manners. He knew the French officers who accompanied M. de Lafayette to America fifty years ago; he has seen M. de Talleyrand—in fact, he is a man of another generation, and time passes quickly in America. The only pleasure I have had since my arrival in this country has been to witness the deep impression M. de Talleyrand left here. On my return to New York I will see Mr. Gallatin, who is still alive; he is eighty years of age, and they say talks a great deal about M. de Talleyrand. Let us go back to the dinner, which was a very bad English dinner, seasoned to the last degree with pepper: the garniture of the table was elegant, but the attendance

very bad, which appears to be the case in every
State in America where slavery has been abolished. They have the greatest difficulty in
finding and keeping servants, or helps, as they
call them. They drank moderately, and the
gentlemen remained but a short time after the
ladies had left the table; but I think that the
presence of three Frenchmen was the cause of
this hasty retreat. At this aristocratic dinner
all the guests were of the opposition party, the
present Administration being purely Democratic.

On leaving the table, I was taken to the garden, where I enjoyed a splendid view. From
the top of a hill covered with beautiful trees,
two hundred feet above the Hudson River, we
could see the whole length of the peninsula of
New York, and in the distance the East River
and Long Island; to the left, ten miles of the
Hudson River flowing majestically through
a well-wooded country; and on the right the
entire bay of New York, enlivened by hundreds
of vessels of every size: this picture was lit up
by a brilliant sun, accompanied by an agreeable sea-breeze.

At nine o'clock I took my leave, returning

by the boat which is used in crossing the North River. We passed through a forest filled with rhododendrons in full flower, which grow here in the woods and fields, over which sparkled as they flew a species of insects called here fireflies, and whose wings are golden. The night was superb; the sky, of a clearness unknown in Europe, became little by little illuminated by stars infinitely more brilliant than in our climate. Before going home we paid a visit to Madame F——, who seemed to me to be singularly attractive to M. de la Forest.

I leave to-morrow for Philadelphia; from there I shall go to Baltimore, where I shall spend the 30th, and arrive in Washington on July 1. I was near forgetting an anecdote characteristic of America which some one told yesterday at table: A girl whose antecedents were bad was married about two years ago in New York and continued in the same course. Her father, in speaking of her, said that she was a worthless person; she brought a suit against him for defamation of character and recovered one thousand dollars damages. They say she has implored her father to continue his abuse of her.

XIII.

PHILADELPHIA, June 27, 1840.

So far, I am not particularly delighted with the American style of travelling, and less so with the arrangements of the hotels: their appearance of cleanliness and elegance impresses you at first sight, but they are wanting in necessary comforts. The furniture is handsome enough, but an easy-chair or a night-table is not to be found, nor in fact are many other articles of the toilet or for one's comfort. If you ask for them, you receive a brutal answer to the effect there are none, and that nobody ever uses such things. The servants are insolent; American travellers never give them any gratuities, and are served accordingly.

Yesterday I went on board the steamboat with all my colony, for we are five— M. de la Fosse, myself, and our servants. We were taken across the river to New Jersey, where we were obliged to make a rush to find places in the *cars of the railroad*, and to contend against that American rudeness which spares no one, except the women, who have a car apart. The American railways are not solid, and are subjected to many accidents; they have the merit of going fast, but this advantage is balanced by numberless inconveniences: the roads are rough; the engines heated by wood, whose flames spread in every direction and often set on fire the woods they pass through; cinders penetrate the *cars*, and at the end of the journey one has the appearance of a coal-heaver. The rapidity with which they travel does not allow them to stop, either to eat or for anything else. Another peculiarity—I suppose owing to their boasted form of government—is the entire absence of all police, and the certainty of being surrounded by thieves; I say the certainty, for there is posted in every corner of every establishment notices containing these words: "Beware of pickpockets," and "The company are not responsible for any robbery." Then, don't forget that all Americans chew tobacco and spit continually around them, and it is difficult to keep out of this filth. A Frenchman who came over with me on the Great Western was robbed of his pocket-book with all his money on the road I went over yesterday; and I have noticed that the Americans, aware of this danger, have their pockets made to open from the inside and not from the outside, as is the custom everywhere else.

The country we have passed through is marshy, with pools and small streams on all sides, flat, badly cultivated, and barren in appearance, and does not improve until you get near Philadelphia, a large city of two hundred and forty thousand inhabitants, which is said to be the most beautiful in the Union. The houses are in fact a little better built than in New York, but always of red brick; the sidewalks are also of brick; there are some handsome edifices in granite. The city seems much quieter and with fewer signs of trade than in New York; it is the scientific capital of the country; they say that the society, being less engrossed in trade, is more agreeable than in other places.

I had engaged rooms at the Union Hotel, through our Consul, M. Maurice d'Hauterive, brother-in-law of M. de la Forest: I expected to find everything comfortably arranged, and have found nothing but a miserable little bedroom, in which I am writing on my knees; they have promised to give me a parlor some time to-day. I went to see M. d'Hauterive, who is said to be an able Consul, but not an amiable man: I had found this out already. I found at his house M. Pageot, until now our chargé d'affaires at Washington; he said he came to meet me, and guarantees me a cordial reception from the Administration, from the Diplomatic Corps, and from the small circle which composes the society there, offering few other resources.

All Philadelphia was astir to see Fanny Elssler, who danced this evening. She is in the same hotel with me. I was much pleased with her dancing, but what amused me as much was to see the hall crowded, and to hear the furious applause, far exceeding London or Paris, and that at Philadelphia, the chief city of the Quakers—Quakers wildly excited over the dancer Fanny Elssler. The theatre is neither large nor well arranged; on the first row were many very pretty women, all young, and dressed so exactly alike, that one would have taken them for sisters had there not been so many of them.

XIV.

June 28, 1840.

I WAS anxious to be settled at Washington, but M. Pageot assured me that it would be very dangerous in my condition of health to live there during the next three months on account of the intense heat. I regret it, as this hotel life is hateful to me. I paid a visit to Madame Pageot, a tall, thin American woman, with an enormous waist, and protruding bad teeth; her husband married her some years ago on account of her great beauty. I made her acquaintance and took my leave of her at the same time. She will remain in Philadelphia until her departure for Europe, which will take place the 1st of August, by the steamboat the British Queen. Her husband accompanies me to Washington to hand over the Legation to me.

Mr. H. Raincy, the most distinguished lawyer in Philadelphia, formerly a member of Congress, to whom Bates had recommended me, has been to see me, and talked a great deal of our dear friend Labouchère.

I have visited the City Hall, and the room

where the famous Declaration of Independence of the colonies then in revolt against England was signed. There is to be seen here a wooden statue of Washington and two full-length portraits — one of Franklin and the other of Lafayette. The most of the signers of the Declaration of Independence were honorable men, who believed they were acting for the good of their country. Since then the times and the men have changed here as with us, where the noble and generous illusions of the members of the Assembly have been replaced by the weakness of the Chamber of Deputies.

On returning to my hotel I called on Mademoiselle Elssler. She kindly expressed regret at not having made the passage across with me. Her performances in the United States are, I think, very successful and remunerative. She does not bear close inspection, and her smile is spoiled by very bad teeth. She remains in Philadelphia a week longer, and will then give four representations at Washington, where I shall see her again. I leave to-morrow morning by steamboat for Baltimore.

XV.

BALTIMORE, June 29, 1840.

YOU see I continue to advance in my journey toward my capital, where I shall be the day after to-morrow at noon. I wish, before taking up my narrative, to thank you for an invitation I received at New York, and which I carelessly forgot to acknowledge. Young Alexander Hamilton, whom you saw at Valençay, brought me, just before I left New York, a very kind letter from his father inviting me to spend a few days at Nevis, where he lives, about twenty-five miles from New York, on the banks of the Hudson. He writes that if his health had not been so bad he should have come to see me in New York, in person immediately on receipt of your letter, being most anxious to obey the wishes of his illustrious friend the Duchess. I thanked young Hamilton very much; he is a young man of polished manners, bright, and speaks French very well. On my return to New York I shall go to Nevis. The family, owing to the memory of the General, is highly

thought of in this country. The Hamilton
you knew in France was a great friend of Mr.
Van Buren, but has become his enemy and
most bitter opponent on account of being
turned out of his place of Collector of Customs in New York, where he had been guilty
of embezzlement of the public money. This,
however, does not injure his reputation here,
but what adds to it is the million of francs
which he acquired during the five years he
occupied his place.* They say his family and
his home are very agreeable; so, thanks for
your kind introduction. The day before yesterday, Sunday, I went to Philadelphia, to a
church constructed on exactly the same plan
as the one in New York; it is the plan common to all the churches here: a long low
building; galleries on each side supported by
wooden columns; at the end one altar only,
without a choir, and the organ above the entrance-door. The service is very well done in
Philadelphia; the music less secular than at

---

* M. de Bacourt evidently confounded Mr. Hamilton
with some other person, as the Mr. Hamilton above referred to never held the office of Collector of Customs of
New York. He was District Attorney under Jackson.

New York, and the men as numerous as the women.

M. d'Hauterive took me to see the city, which is beautiful, and would be more so without the bright-red color of the bricks. All the frames of the doors and windows are of white marble, as are also the door-steps. The streets, which are regular and at right angles, are planted with trees. I saw Washington Square, which is the elegant square; then Franklin Square, which is the popular one: they are very pretty, with fountains and beautiful trees. The common people who walk in them, notwithstanding the solemnity of Sunday, are not at all rough. I saw also a superb covered market, one mile and a half in length, remarkably well kept. Philadelphia resembles my dear cities of Holland: the same regularity, verdure everywhere, and the same death-like silence. M. d'Hauterive says that the society here is really distinguished. He spoke to me of a woman of great intelligence bearing the grotesque name of "Cigogne!" A French creole by birth, she came here after the disasters in our colonies, and established a boarding-school, in which for the last thirty years all the young girls of the best society have been educated. She holds the highest position in society here, and gives parties and dinners—all this, of course, aside from her school, which continues its routine, and with which she occupies herself in her leisure hours. My predecessor, M. Pontois, visited her often, and as she has expressed a wish to see me, it is agreed that I shall be presented to her on my next visit to Philadelphia.

I went with M. Pageot on board of a steamboat, which took us down the Delaware River to French Town, a little village, where we left our boat and were taken by railroad, in one hour, to Elk Town, another small village on the shores of the Chesapeake, a bay celebrated in the records of American Independence. There we took another boat, which carried us to Baltimore. All these transshipments were made with incredible rapidity and order, no noise and no embarrassment, and the boats are excellent and well managed.

I talked a great deal during the journey with M. Pageot, who gave me a great deal of information about the details of my Legation and the organization of my household. It seems that the great difficulty of the Mission is to find matter for dispatches. M. Pageot has a sound understanding, but his intelligence has been blunted by a residence here of ten years. He goes back to Europe very much discontented with his long exile. He pursued his journey to Washington, where he will be kind enough to arrange for my accommodation at the hotel. I have stopped here at a large hotel called "*Exchange House,*" built by Jerome Bonaparte, son of Miss Patterson, who is married, and lives in Baltimore.

After dinner I received the Count de Menou, formerly Secretary of the French Legation at Washington, deprived of his place under the Restoration for not having once written to his Government during eighteen months that he had been chargé d'affaires to the United States. He is reduced to extreme poverty, and does anything he can for a living. I have promised him the same assistance that my predecessors have given him. He has an original mind, knows the country well, and has already furnished me with a great amount of information. In the evening he took me to see the city, which contains more than one hundred thousand inhabitants. Not so beautiful as Philadelphia, and situated in the form of an amphitheatre. There are some large monuments here, amongst others the column erected in memory of General Washington, by the State of Maryland. This column, of white marble, surmounted by the statue of the General, looks like an organ-pipe. Another was erected in honor of the Americans killed near the city in 1814, in the war against the English. The cathedral so much talked of is abominable. It is a mosque, with a dome like a rotunda, and with hideous minarets, built half of granite and half of brick, forming the ensemble of a *plat monté*. The architecture in the United States is detestable.

Just now financial disasters are at their height in Baltimore. Men who were rich yesterday are beggars to-day! This town is the seat of an archbishopric. There is also here a Sulpician seminary and a convent of the Visitation. After having paid my visit to the archbishop, I visited the seminary. This proceeding, of which I spoke to M. de Menou, astonished him. He said that it would produce a very good effect. I replied that it was not done with that intention, but to gratify myself. This increased his astonishment.

The State of Maryland, in which I am now, is a slave State; consequently the negroes are more numerous here and more polite than in those States where slavery has been abolished. I can scarcely accustom myself to their black and oily faces. They inspire me with a repulsion, perhaps unjust, but unconquerable.

I saw yesterday a very curious animal which is called the sloth: it is something between the cat and the monkey, and therefore not handsome. He climbs a tree and eats the leaves, then lets himself fall to the ground from pure laziness, where he remains in a state of torpor until he is roused again by hunger. The one I saw seemed very *cross* at being chained. I see here magnificent trees that in Europe would be but miserable shrubs —such as the catalpa, the sugar-maple, the rhododendron, etc., etc.

If it were not for my bad health I should take a much stronger interest in all these things, so new to me; but suffering gives a discolored view to everything, and I feel as *cross* as the "sloth," and kept back, like him, by a chain the weight of which overpowers me.

The prices in the hotels everywhere in America are exorbitant. Although living moderately, I cannot manage to spend less than twenty dollars a day.

XVI.

BALTIMORE, June 30, 1840.

I HAVE just returned from a visit to the archbishop, who received me very well; he is a handsome man, of forty years of age at most, who has the best manners I have yet seen in an American. An old Sulpician, he passed, ten years ago, two years at Issy, near Paris; he speaks French very well, and inquired with much interest about the Christian end of M. de Talleyrand's life, which until now he appears not to have credited. But he was delighted with what I told him of it, and begged me to repeat it to the director of his seminary, whom I am to visit this evening, and who, it seems, attaches a great importance to this affair. We also spoke of M. de Forbin-Janson, who has been in the United States for the last eight months. I profited by this occasion to beg the archbishop to prevail upon M. de Janson to speak more moderately about France and its present Government, for I have heard that in New York and in New Orleans he had expressed himself in the pulpit in the most violent manner against us, accusing us of being atheists. The archbishop took what I said in good part, and replied, "M. de Janson is a man of intelligence, but too ardent; he is wrong in introducing politics in his sermons: I always avoid it, even in this country, where priests have a right to say what they please. Although born in America and as good a republican as any one, I do not vote, and never try to influence my parishioners as to how they shall vote; it would only be in case the liberty of my religion was threatened that I should assert my right as an American citizen. I have already requested M. de Forbin-Janson to be more moderate, but it is not to be wondered at that he should sometimes wander from his subject, for he preaches too much. Just imagine! —he has preached two hundred times in four months. He is very wrong in attacking the King of the French. This sovereign has shown himself favorable to religion, and since he commenced his reign has made none but excellent choice of bishops, etc., etc."

The archbishop spoke also of the progress of Catholicism in America, and even in the State of Massachusetts, where thirty years ago there were not ten Catholic families: now there are forty Catholic churches and a bishop at Boston, the most puritanical city in the United States. There are numerous conversions everywhere, and almost all the Irish and German emigrants are Catholic. This progress has been apparent in New England also, where the Protestants are so ardently zealous. There are in the United States fourteen bishops, and they talk of creating two new seats; the Catholic population will soon reach a million. The increased number of bishops and the building of churches are facts more remarkable because the revenues of the clergy and the church are covered by subscriptions and the rent of the seats in the churches.

The archbishop took me into his cathedral, the interior of which is in as bad taste as the exterior; but he is very proud of this monument, which has cost the Catholics a great deal of money.

I have just returned, roasted and boiled. Ah, what heat under " this beautiful sky"!

XVII.

WASHINGTON CITY, July 2, 1840.

THIS time, I write to you from my capital—or I should say better from my *penitentiary*.

The day before yesterday, before leaving Baltimore, I went with the Count de Menou to visit the Seminary of Saint-Sulpice, which is composed of ten priests, five of whom are French, and thirteen pupils. The college, which adjoins it and is under the direction of the same priests, has three hundred pupils, one half of whom are Protestants. The Abbé Chauch, who is the head of the college, was born in Baltimore. He is a distinguished man in his conversation and manners. The seminary was founded in 1791 by five French Sulpicians who came to the United States to escape persecution ; they have had to contend against a thousand difficulties, which they have overcome with great courage, and later were able to found the college which is more prosperous than the seminary, for which they could only get recruits from foreigners. Americans have little taste for a life of meditation : their feverish activity ill fits them for a uniform and peaceful life.

The principal of the seminary is the Abbé Delnot ; born in the Vivarais, he came here twenty-five years ago. Although less distinguished than the Abbé Chauch, I think he is, notwithstanding his common appearance, an able man. He was very much interested in the Christian death of M. de Talleyrand ; he had already been informed of what I had said on the subject to Monseigneur Eccleston in the morning ; it delighted him. He spoke with much feeling of the Saint-Sulpice in Paris, of the Abbé Garnier, of M. Emmery, etc. ... These good priests showed me every detail of their seminary, the college, and their little chapel in the Gothic style, which is far better than the cathedral. They related to me a very singular fact concerning the establish-

ment of Catholic bishoprics in the United
States: the promoter of the foundation of the
first seat was Jefferson, who was said to be an
unbeliever in any religion. Observing the
tendency of the American Catholics to follow
the English Catholic Church, even after their
separation from the mother Church, he
thought this might produce trouble, and
whilst Minister at Paris in 1789, having induced the American Government to adopt his
views, he was authorized to negotiate with
the Papal Nuncio and obtained the creation of
a bishopric at Baltimore; which thus became
the head of the Church in the United States,
and will soon have fifteen assistant bishops.

M. de Menou says that the bishop was
much pleased with my visit. He took it for
granted that I acted in my official capacity,
and from instructions given by the king: I
begged M. de Menou to assure him that I had
acted entirely from personal feeling.

I left Baltimore yesterday, and the railroad
brought us to Washington in two hours and
a half, through a beautiful wooded country,
more thickly inhabited than any I have seen
yet. M. Pageot and the Count de Mon-

tholon, my paid attaché, met me and took me to Gadsby's Hotel, where I am installed for a fortnight. M. Pageot has written to the Secretary of State to ask him when he would wish to receive me. One hour afterward he received a reply from M. Forsyth saying he would see me to-day at noon. I shall then know on what day I can present my letters of credit to the President. I invited these gentlemen to dine with me. M. Montholon has very simple manners, quiet and polished, and talks very sensibly; he is even thinner than I am. My predecessor, M. Pontois, has an idea that M. de Montholon's title of Count places him (Pontois) in an inferior position in the eyes of the Americans, so impressed are they by titles.

As I was going out with these gentlemen I met at the door the Baron de Mareschall, the Austrian Minister, who had very kindly come to see me, although it was not his place to make the first visit : he invited me and all my Legation to dine with him to-day. He remembered having met me two years ago at the Princess of Schönbourg's house, who had been kind enough, as also had the Countess

Appony, to write very amiably about me; consequently he expressed frankly a wish to establish intimate relations between us. He is said to be the most distinguished man of the Diplomatic Corps; he appears to be about fifty years of age, and has seen a great deal of service in the army and in diplomacy; he was born in the Duchy of Luxembourg when that country was Austrian. We visited the town, which is really composed of but one street, called Pennsylvania Avenue, which runs from east to west, it is three miles long: at one end is the Capitol, the most beautiful building in the United States; at the other is the President's House, surrounded by all the public offices. The avenue is crossed by streets at right angles, in each of which are only five or six houses; there are other streets radiating toward the President's House, but not much more built upon than the cross streets; so that on all sides you can reach the open country in five hundred steps. The avenue is half as large again as the Rue de la Paix; it is planted with trees, and adorned with brick sidewalks; the middle, macadamized, and never being watered, is in summer a terrible mass of dust and in winter a common sewer.

The other streets are not paved, but have sidewalks. The appearance of the city is quite pretty at this season on account of the verdure, but when the trees have lost their leaves it must be even more gloomy than Carlsruhe. The houses have but one story above the ground-floor, are all of red brick, and have a mean appearance; they are too much spread out for their twenty-five thousand inhabitants.

XVIII.

WASHINGTON, July 3, 1840.

IT is very difficult to find a house in this charming country: the finished houses are either occupied by their owners, or by tenants who have engaged them some time before, and take possession as soon as the builders have left. The home of my predecessor does not suit me at all: there are no furniture-dealers, and I can neither buy furniture nor rent it, so that I shall have to be contented with living in a furnished house, and have my meals brought to me. There are two Frenchmen here who furnish lodging and board to families without a home, or to a poor devil like myself, who does not know where to stow himself. One of these men has a good house, but having made his fortune, is insolent, negligent, and dirty. The house of the other is small and badly furnished; but as he has his fortune to make, and I shall have the pleasure of contributing to it, he will perhaps be docile and attentive. I am in favor of this latter, whose name is Galbrun. I made an arrangement with a livery-stable keeper to furnish me with a carriage and horses; the bargain was completed, but this morning he came to tell me that I must not count on him unless I paid him one third more than the price agreed upon. In this country they take back their word without ceremony; no contract is respected unless it is signed.

We went yesterday with M. Pageot to Mr. Forsyth's, the Palmerston of this country, who has the reputation of being very stiff, impolite, and cynical; however, he received me very well, and tried to overcome the coldness of his naturally unamiable manner; but it was evident that it was an effort. After having paid a visit to M. Vail, whom you knew in

London, and who is about to leave here for Madrid, I went to dine with Baron Mareschall, who had invited to meet me Mr. Forsyth, Secretary of State;—Mr. Fox, the English Minister, who is an oddity. He has a great deal of wit, but affects great eccentricity; although young, he appears from his dress and carriage to be at least fifty years old;—the Minister of Russia, M. Bodisco, who is quite a character. I knew him in Stockholm. Just the reverse of Mr. Fox, he tries to appear young: eighteen years ago I left him with gray hair, and I find him with black curly hair, and whiskers and mustache dyed; at sixty years of age he has just married an American girl of sixteen! Great good may it do him! He is in fact ridiculous, vulgar, and disgusting. I was told that he was in great fear of me, which does not astonish me, for he knows that I am well acquainted with his antecedents;—M. Martini, Minister from Holland, an inoffensive man, and *very indifferent;*—and last, M. Vail and my Legation. After dinner we played whist. At the hotel I found a letter announcing that the President would receive me to-morrow at two o'clock.

XIX.

WASHINGTON, July 4, 1840.

TO-DAY is the great National holiday—the anniversary of the Declaration of Independence, sixty-four years ago. It is celebrated in every part of America, if not with suitable splendor, at least with a prodigious noise; they say that it is not safe to be in New York to-day, but here it is less noisy, and without danger.

I went to see the President yesterday before two o'clock in the house which is called *Execution Mansion*, a pretty palace, surrounded by a garden in English style and an iron fence; the rooms are large and well decorated. The Secretary of State, who ought to have presented me, had not arrived; few minutes after my arrival I saw Mr. Van Buren enter. I scarcely recognized him, he had grown so fat. He wore a plain black coat and gray trousers and boots; this entirely consoled me for not having my uniform, which has not yet arrived.

After the ceremony of reception, Mr. Van Buren took me by the hand and led me to a sofa ; he said he was delighted to see me, and had not forgotten our meeting in London. He asked very particularly about you, and questioned me in the kindliest manner about the death of M. de Talleyrand. The audience was very long, and Mr. Van Buren spoke in the most charming manner of the king and of France, etc. ... M. Pageot, who was present, said that during the ten years he had been here he had never seen so cordial a reception. I have left cards on all the members of Congress. The election for President will take place in five months ; they say that the election of Mr. Van Buren would be a calamity to the country, because he is the chief of an ultra-Democratic Party. I forgot to tell you that Mr. Van Buren is called the American Talleyrand. This must flatter him, for in talking to me of the dear Prince he repeated at least ten times *wonderful man*. Mr. Van Buren is acknowledged to be a very able man, but more in what concerns his personal affairs than in the direction of the affairs of the country.

XX.

WASHINGTON, July 5, 1840.

I HAVE concluded my arrangements with Galbrun, who boasts of having worked for two years in the kitchen of M. de Talleyrand, under the superintendence of Louis Esbrat; he engages, in renting me the house, to furnish food, heat, light, etc..., for M. de la Fosse, myself, and all my servants, for three hundred dollars a month; this arrangement is not entirely satisfactory, but I shall be free from the troubles of keeping house; I cannot take posession for three months yet; until then I must put up with hotel life.

I paid about forty visits with M. Pageot to the Diplomatic Corps and to some of the Senators, on whom, according to custom here, the foreign Ministers must call first. I only found M. Martini and M. Bodisco, who live in Georgetown, a small town forming part of Washington, but two miles distant from it. I have also seen Mr. Clay, a Senator and head of the opposition party, the great orator of the country; his proclivities are very French.

I was not able, in an interview of only a few minutes, to form any opinion, except from his exterior, which is that of an English farmer. He received me cordially, and invited me to pay him a visit some time in the summer, at his country place in Kentucky, six hundred miles from here.

I have been at an evening party at Mr. Paulding's: I only stayed half an hour, but this half-hour sufficed for ten or twelve *introductives*—the most tedious drudgeries of a Minister's début. One must endeavor to recollect the faces and the names, then to put the names on the faces; it keeps one's mind constantly occupied by the fear of mistakes. I saw Madame Bodisco, who has the beauty of youth and a silly manner. Mr. and Mrs. Paulding, the master and mistress of the house, are old people, perfectly insignificant, and the rest of the company appeared exactly like the society one meets in every town in America—*English people of second and third rate.* I may find my first impression incorrect, when I have talked more with some distinguished persons and become more intimate.

The little Catholic Church, of which I am a

parishioner, is neat and well kept; the Mass which I attended, although Low Mass, lasted more than an hour on account of a short sermon and of the great number of communicants, the half of whom at least were negroes and negresses. The French Legation has a pew, for which it pays yearly; eight days before my arrival, the curé sent to M. Pageot for the rent due, and a message by the beadle to say that the pew would be of no use to me as I was a Protestant; they read that in a newspaper. On this authority M. Pageot believed it to be so, and told several persons. You see that news false or true is spread in the same way on both sides of the Atlantic. This reminds me to tell you that M. de la Fosse is a Calvinist; but we shall never dispute about religion.

In the middle of the day the heat is overpowering, but the nights and mornings cold.

XXI.

I HAVE continued my visits to the members of the Senate; I saw Mr. Benton, who is a violent Democrat, one of the principal upholders of the Administration, and a particular friend of Mr. Van Buren; they say he is well-informed, eloquent, and clever; he is Senator from the State of Missouri, which was formed from part of Louisiana, the population is partly French; his home is near St. Louis, where he passes his vacations, *at a thousand miles* from here—a mere nothing! He talked a great deal about the moral and religious state of the old population of Louisiana, who appear to have pursued a course the reverse of that of Canada, where they are incrusted with the manners and customs of sixty years ago; in Louisiana, on the contrary, the people have become quick and intelligent in mixing with the Anglo-Americans; they are richer, more moral and honest, and rival them in activity. Mr. Benton also says that in all the new States in the West there is a large number of Protestants who have been converted to the Catholic

Church, on account of the doubts caused by the infinite number of Protestant sects. Young Protestants are educated in Catholic schools; their parents confide them with a feeling of perfect security to the integrity and enlightenment of the Catholic clergy of America.

I have visited the city more thoroughly; the exterior of the President's house is the best I have seen in America; this pretty palace has a circular front supported by columns opening on the garden and on the country. From there you have an extended view of the course of the Potomac; the *pleasure-ground* is well laid out, kept in good order, and open to the public; it is a handsome place, and from it very little can be seen of the so-called city of Washington, which is neither city nor village: it is a collection of houses put anywhere and everywhere with no regularity; it has a miserable, desolate look, even with the foliage; what must it be when covered with snow and ice!

XXII.

WASHINGTON, July 7, 1840.

As I advance I find my troubles and vexation increase without the least compensation. Later, when I am more accustomed to the habits and manners of the country, I shall be able to give you an account of my observations, but at present I fear my judgment would be too hasty. I do not wish to imitate some of my compatriots, who at the end of eight days had judged everything, and habitually condemned all they saw.

This is the forty-fifth day since the packet-boat left Havre with all my baggage on board, and I hear nothing of her. It seems that except in spring, and sometimes autumn, when the winds are favorable, no one can count with any certainty upon the duration of a voyage of a sailing-vessel.

M. Pageot is so much wounded by the neglect with which he has been treated in leaving him here to languish without the slightest acknowledgment of his services, that he has decided to send in his resignation, expressed in rather sharp terms. I advised him very strongly not to do so, and tried to soothe him; but in vain. I appreciate his ability and his services; no one knows the country better; his correspondence is excellent, and he has been successful in his treatment of some very difficult questions; but for all that he has not been able to obtain justice. One must have good luck to succeed: sometimes bad luck may, as mine in sending me here.

I have been to a meeting of Congress. The Capitol, where they hold these meetings, is a beautiful edifice situated on a height; it commands a very extended view of the pretty valley of the Potomac. This building is divided into three distinct parts: in the centre is a rotunda with a glazed cupola to give light to the interior; the principal entrance leads directly into this rotunda, the proportions of which are beautiful. Opposite the entrance door is the library; on the right the Senate Chamber; on the left that of the Representatives. The distribution of the two halls is the same as that of our Chamber of Deputies, only smaller; the ornamentation is simple, and in good taste. In the Senate Chamber there is only one portrait—that of General Washington; in the other Chamber you also find one of Washington, but with one of La Fayette as a pendant. Whatever may have been the wrongs attributed to La Fayette, his portrait hung in the Hall of the House of Representatives is undoubtedly an honorable tribute to his memory.

In the Rotunda there are twelve framed spaces ready for pictures, but as yet four only are filled. The first painting represents the Declaration of Independence in 1776; the second, the defeat at Saratoga in 1777, where the English General Burgoyne gave up his sword to General Washington; the third, a review after the victory of Yorktown: the French and American troops occupy the two sides of the picture—the French with their white cockades and their white flag, with Marshal Rochambeau at their head; the Americans commanded by M. de La Fayette; in the centre is General Washington: the fourth and last represents the meeting of Congress, at which General Washington resigns the command of the army. As paintings, these tableaux are neither better nor worse than those we saw on our visit to Versailles three months ago.

The two Houses were in session: the Senate, which is composed of fifty-two members, conduct themselves with great propriety. I cannot say as much for the House of Representatives. I do not speak of the custom, imported from England, of keeping their hats on, but many of the members sit with their legs in the air, and others, stretched out, sleep as if they were in their beds. What shocked me most was the sound of continual spitting: this filthy habit is common to both Houses, as well as to every man in the country; they all spit—everywhere and on anything. This is the consequence of the villainous habit of chewing tobacco; the President is the only one I have seen who is exempt from this vice. They say that there are several distinguished orators in the Senate; none of them spoke yesterday, but I shall hear them next winter, for it seems that the sessions of Congress are the great and only attraction here.

In the Senate Chamber I was introduced to Mr. Buchanan, formerly American Minister to Russia, who remembers having dined at London with Prince Talleyrand, you, and myself, at the Princess Lieven's. I also made the acquaintance of my colleague the Minister of Prussia, M. de Roün, who arrived only two days ago. He spoke very amiably of having received a dispatch from M. de Werther, who congratulated him on the prospect of meeting me, and added that I had left many regrets at Carlsruhe; I thoroughly reciprocate this sentiment.

The library at the Capitol, which contains twenty thousand volumes, is at the disposition of the Diplomatic Corps.

I met M. de Mareschall in the street. The more I see of him the less I like him: he is a great gossip and sneers at everything; this is perhaps the effect of his long stay here, and makes me tremble for myself.

XXIII.

WASHINGTON, July 11, 1840.

I PAID a visit to my curé yesterday. He is American by birth, but brought up in Liege; he returned to America during the French Revolution. He came to Washington, which was being built, and, thinking that it would become a city of importance, bought a large tract of land; during the last thirty-five years, by the aid of subscriptions from Catholics, he has erected on this land a pretty church, a presbytery, a small hospital where the Sisters of Charity take care of the sick, and a school where fifty poor children are educated gratuitously. The Abbé Matteus seems to me to be a good honest man, distinguished only for his charity—perhaps the highest of all distinctions. He told me that there were now in Washington three churches and more than six thousand Catholics; that is, one third of the whole population.

I dined with the President this evening. We sat down at seven o'clock, and left the table at ten! It was hard work. As the dinner was given to me, I had the place of honor, although the whole Diplomatic Corps were present; it is a compliment always paid here to the last comer. When dinner was announced the President took my arm and escorted me to the dining-room, a handsome room and well decorated, and placed me on his right. The table with forty covers would have sufficed for a hundred guests. The service, for America, was elegant, and the dinner good. The French cook told my footman a curious fact. He said: "For several months, during which the question of the re-election of Mr. Van Buren has been agitated, people had come constantly to see him, and in the rudest manner insisted upon being asked to breakfast or dinner, threatening in case of refusal to vote against him. The cook says that he has the greatest difficulty in satisfying them; that they often send back what he serves them, and order other dishes on the pretext that the first were bad." So, said my servant gravely, "It seems that it is not very pleasant to be President!"

Mr. Van Buren has been very kind and polite to me; he told me that he was always at home in the evening, and would be delighted to see me often. He is a widower, with four sons: the oldest is married; his wife is at a watering-place. Mr. Van Buren, the son of an innkeeper, and himself, even, trained to the family calling, has acquired to an astonishing degree the ways of the world; he is a man of polished manners, and has a certain ease which gives him a superiority, as a man of the world, over any of his compatriots whom I have yet seen.

There were at this dinner, besides the Diplomatic Corps, the Cabinet, the heads of the Administration, and several Senators of the Opposition, amongst others Mr. Clay, who is the leader. I made the acquaintance of Mr. Woodbury, Secretary of the Navy—*insignificant;* and that of Mr. Poinsett, Secretary of War, who pleased me tolerably well: he knows Europe, and speaks French well. I prefer him infinitely to Mr. Forsyth, who, it is said, treats everything as a joke, and is not pleasant to deal with.

The evening was magnificent, and the scene before the President's House, with the silver light of the moon upon it, was splendid. The sky in this country is purer than any ever seen in our hemisphere.

XXIV.

WASHINGTON, July 12, 1840.

I HAD the most stupid dinner in the world at M. Bodisco's, and probably presented the most ridiculous figure. Invited at seven o'clock, we sat down to dinner at eight, after having seen the master of the house run in and out several times as though he was preparing this execrable repast which he had the goodness to offer us. He then crowded us, thirty-six in number, into a very small dining-room, where we suffocated until eleven o'clock. I was seated between Mrs. Forsyth, who talked to me in English, and her daughter Mrs. Shaaff, who spoke French, both talking at the same time! I was too uncomfortable to speak any language. This dinner was the perfection of the ridiculous: the table loaded with china, glass, and bronzes of no value and in bad taste, spread out for ornament, not for use. The guests laughed at their host in the most open manner, and every one pitied the unhappy child who had become the wife of this villanous old man.

Having exhausted all the reading matter I had brought with me from Paris, I begged M. de Montholon to lend me a book. He brought me "Travels in America," by M. de Chateaubriand, who embarked at Saint-Malo May 6, 1791, with five Sulpicians, founders of the establishment which I visited lately. The work is not worth much as an account of his journey; and I agree with M. de Tocqueville, who said to me that M. de Chateaubriand had not seen all the places he wrote about—particularly the Mississippi, which he has pictured as superb.

I called on M. Miollet, but did not find him at home. He is the man on whom I count most here, although I have only exchanged a bow with him in the street. He was mathematician and astronomer at the Observatory in Paris, a rival of M. Arago. He left France during the Revolution of July—some said on account of his opinions, others thought because he had lost his fortune; whatever it was, he took refuge in the United States, where he has acquired great distinction. He has done important work for the American Government, and no one knows the country better than he does. He has been everywhere, often living in the woods with the Indians. They say it is very interesting to hear him talk. So much for the savant. As a man he is esteemed even more highly; modest, simple, and obliging, every one aspires to gain his friendship; in fact he has a great reputation, and is exceptionally esteemed.

I went last night to see Fanny Elssler dance the Tarentella and the Cachucha; she danced ravishingly, and was applauded with frenzy.

M. de la Fosse told me this morning, speaking of M. de Chateaubriand, that he had seen a very curious letter of this *great genius*, in his own handwriting, signed, and addressed by him to M. de Talleyrand, then at the Congress of Vienna, consequently written between the months of October, 1814, and March, 1815. In this tolerably long letter M. de Chateaubriand complained of the proceedings of the Government, particularly of its ingratitude toward himself, and he announced his intention to enter the diplomatic service of some foreign power, thinking by this means he would succeed better in making his fortune. A very short answer from M. de Talleyrand in his own handwriting was attached to this letter—merely a simple acknowledgment of its receipt, and making no allusion to his announced intention of entering a foreign service. M. de la Fosse, who had come across these letters in reading the correspondence of the Congress of Vienna when he was attached to the Ministry of Foreign Affairs in 1835, thought M. de Chateaubriand's letter so extraordinary that he showed it to several of his young colleagues, and afterward took it to M. de Viel-Castel, who had never heard of it, and was very much astonished. M. de Viel-Castel had the custody of the portfolio in which these letters were kept. Some days afterward, M. de la Fosse, while continuing his examination of the documents contained in this volume, looked for the letter, wishing to read it again: it had disappeared. He supposed then, and still thinks, that M. de Viel-Castel either returned the letter to M. de Chateaubriand, with whom he had been associated, or had kept it for himself as a curious record.

XXV.

WASHINGTON, July 17, 1840.

I DINED yesterday with Mr. Forsyth. Pepper sauces seasoned with a thousand American perfumes and an atrocious heat! The usual hour for dinner here is four o'clock, but when any one is invited to dinner it is at seven by *fashion!* The service is so very slow at a dinner of ceremony, on account of an insufficient number of servants, that one is obliged to remain at table three or four hours. I was in the place of honor next to the mistress of the house, and had the daughter-in-law on the other side. I am anxious to lose my position as débutant, that I may be able to feel more at my ease, at some obscure corner of the table.

I am writing to you at last from home. I I am very uncomfortably settled, wanting many necessary things, but they are unknown here. My house is like a parrot's perch; they are all built on the same plan, both inconvenient and ugly; nevertheless I am *at home*, and happy to be for the present free from that horrid hotel life.

I saw Madame de Montholon yesterday, who has just recovered from a confinement. Her face, which is rather sweet than pretty, is already faded, like that of all the young American women, and she is not twenty years old.

I went also to see the President, who appears troubled. He probably has bad news in regard to the election. M. Pageot, who leaves Washington to-day, has taken his leave of him.

Fanny Elssler came to see me while I was out. She continues to appear here every night, and is received with the same furore.

I made the acquaintance of Mr. Robinson, a civil engineer, and a distinguished man; he is a friend of Michel Chevalier, who gave me a letter for him. He lives in Philadelphia.

I have begun to put the books of the Chancellerie in order. They have been kept very badly, and I wish to leave the archives in as good order as those I left in London and Carlsruhe.

XXVI.

WASHINGTON, July 18, 1840.

I HAVE just returned from a visit to Fanny Elssler, who has engaged a kind of duenna whom she could dispense with very well, for the poor girl's reputation is too far gone to be benefited by a guardian. I am wrong in saying poor, for she has made a great deal of money here; so much that, since she has heard her engagement at the Opera in Paris has been broken by the retirement of M. Duponchel, she is strongly tempted to remain for a year in America. If she does, she will go this winter to New Orleans and Havana and pocket all the money she can. Just imagine—she was presented formally to the President, and to all the Cabinet assembled to receive her. This strikes me as the height of the ridiculous! She is delighted with her reception everywhere, and said, in a very droll way, that what surprised her most was to find the manners of Mr. Van Buren as distinguished as those of Metternich.

I met at a dinner at the Belgian Minister's,

Mr. King, Senator from Alabama and Vice-President of the Senate; Mr. Calhoun, another Senator; and Mr. Gilpin, Attorney-General.

I also made the acquaintance of M. Miollet, an excellent and remarkable man, whose conversation is charming. He has passed four years amongst the Indians, and talks in the most interesting manner about these unhappy people

---

XXVII.

WASHINGTON, July 21, 1840.

I WENT this morning to say good-by to Fanny Elssler, who is going to Baltimore; she told me all about her love affairs. M. de la Valette is the favored lover, but he is at Pau just now. I think he was wrong in letting her go without him. Before leaving, he had recommended her to an American who was a friend of his, Mr. Wickoff, who accompanied her to America and follows her everywhere. She spoke to me of La Valette as her lover and Mr. Wickoff as her friend; I took all that for what it is worth.

I went to Congress twice yesterday; they were obliged to sit all night, and the session finishes to-day. I am afraid that it may finish badly for us: the Government have proposed a bill taxing our silks—which have been allowed to enter free of duty for many years—ten per cent. If this bill passes, it will make a bad début for me in my mission, although I have been here too short a time to be accused of negligence.

XXVIII.

WASHINGTON, July 23, 1840.

I WAS present at the closing of the session of Congress. They adjourned without having passed the terrible bill taxing our silks, but it will pass without a doubt at the next session. I have written a long dispatch giving an account of all I could gather, and announcing my intention of travelling during the next two months. M. de la Fosse does not wish to accompany me, so I go alone.

I have received my first letters from Europe after waiting fifty-seven days for them.

XXIX.

PHILADELPHIA, July 26, 1840.

I LEFT Washington yesterday by the railroad, which brought me to Baltimore in three hours, where Fanny Elssler gave a representation. They say that this lovely creature has married M. Wickoff. It will be an excellent match for her; it is true he is a bastard, but he has sixty thousand francs a year. I arrived here early, and leave to-morrow.

XXX.

NEW YORK, July 28, 1840.

I AM in a city that I do not like; I do things that do not amuse me, and I am lodged in a place that does not please me.

Yesterday afternoon I walked about the streets of this noisy city. First I met a procession of a thousand Democrats,—that is to say, friends of Mr. Van Buren,—yelling furiously and obstructing the streets. I escaped toward the Battery in the hope of enjoying the sunset

on the sea. I hardly reached there when I
saw several men engaged in a quarrel; they
were dressed like gentlemen,—all the men are
equally well-dressed here,—but that did not
prevent them from tearing each other's hair and
fighting like porters, as they probably were: a
great crowd collected, and I hurried away from
the brutal spectacle.

I shall go to-morrow to New Brighton, opposite New York, and spend two or three days
with M. and Madame Pageot before their departure for Europe; one can go by water in
half an hour.

XXXI.

NEW YORK, July 29, 1840.

STATEN ISLAND, where we are now staying,
which is called the Pavilion of New Brighton,
would be even in Europe a magnificent establishment; I have not seen in any of the watering-places that I have been to anything equal
to it. It is a succession of charming pavilions
built on the shore opposite New York, and
from each of which one enjoys a beautiful

view of the harbor. The parlors, dining-rooms, and bedrooms are very pleasant, and the food is good; the *company* is very mixed. However, I have found some persons who may be agreeable companions. I was presented to Madame d'Argaiz, wife of the Spanish Minister, who is forty years old, and still has beautiful black eyes. She is said to be clever, coquettish, and witty; she passes the summer here, but during the winter she keeps open house in Washington; her husband is a nephew of D'Alava. There is also here a General d' Alvear, Minister of the Republic of Buenos-Ayres and Chargé d'Affaires of Brazil. I have been walking with M. and Madame Pageot all the evening on the beach under a star-lit sky, such as is never seen in Europe. Madame Pageot, who, like all Americans, is very ambitious, feels very much the neglect her husband has suffered in his career; it was she who induced him to send his resignation, and she is anxious that he should become a deputy of the Opposition.

XXXII.

New Brighton, July 31, 1840.

Notwithstanding the beauty of the place, this aimless life is hateful to me. All these unknown faces, these children crying in every part of the house, these *misses* who will play the piano at all times—all this is very unpleasant and annoying. After dinner M. and Madame Pageot, M. Menou, and I drove along the shore to the telegraph which signals the arrival of vessels coming to New York. The view from this point is admirable: on the left is a place called "Quarantine," where twenty merchant-vessels were at anchor; they had come from the South and were waiting for permission to enter the harbor; opposite is the island of Long Island, with its well laid-out grounds; in the middle of the sea Fort Hamilton, which defends the entrance of the harbor; on the right the open sea; behind us Staten Island, on which are the Pavilion of New Brighton, and an infinity of villas and cottages, all surrounded by verdure.

The life Americans lead in a place like this

is really curious: the women remain in their bedrooms during the entire morning; some of the men go to their business in New York; others sleep or play billiards; eighty people sit down to dinner and hurry through it in about half an hour; then the women go back to their rooms, where they remain until tea-time. During this interval the men go to a sort of café, which they call *bar-rooms* here, and smoke and drink and play. Notwithstanding this kind of life, I think the Americans make very good husbands, treating their wives with care: they always give them the best places, and the choice bits at table. This is done without affectation, as a matter of right, and not of homage; treating them with undoubted politeness, but with perfect indifference.

The more intimately I am thrown with Americans the more difficult I find it to judge them, owing to their different types. The American of the North differs entirely from one of the South—I mean only the North and South of the United States. The American of the North, he who is called *Yankee*, has the English type, together with the cunning and skill of the Jew. This mixture of Britannic pride, coldness, and stiffness with the Hebraic cunning makes of the Yankee a being apart.

The Yankees are English at heart, in spite of the contempt they profess for them. They go to England to acquire their tastes, their morals, their customs, their fashions, and to encourage their antipathies to France and the French. Much more civilized than their compatriots of the South, they sympathize with aristocracy and all other superiority admitted in England; and in what they call the New England States very little change is required to establish a form of government altogether like that of Old England. On the contrary, in the Southern States their sympathies are French; but I am sorry to say it is only our revolutionary ideas they sympathize with. They are vain, and jealous of the civilization of the North, whom they would like to crush with their principles of extreme democracy. Such are the two distinct races, who together occupy the territory on the shores of the United States which extend from the North to the South. But there is a third race, in the West, beyond the Alleghany Mountains, on the banks of the Ohio, the Mississippi, and Missouri: this race has separate characteristics, which it would be difficult to describe now; the population is composed of emigrants from the Northern and Southern States, from Ireland, and from Germany. In my opinion the West will be called upon to play the principal rôle in the United States. Some years from now they will dominate the two other sections. It is difficult to say what it will become, for it is composed just now of so heterogeneous a mixture that no one can form an exact idea of the situation; but amongst the different elements which can and ought to be developed, I consider that the Catholic element will exercise the most marked influence.

It seems to me that most writers on America and Americans do not sufficiently consider the time and circumstances. The Anglo-American race is, in my opinion, charged with a special providential mission—that of peopling and civilizing this immense continent; they are proceeding in the accomplishment of this work undisturbed by any obstacle, and this explains the anomalies so easy to observe and criticise. But it is not fair to judge from details: one must see the whole, and this whole is grand, majestic, and imposing.

And is it not imposing to see a nation who sixty years ago numbered three million settled upon the shores of the Atlantic, increase to eighteen millions, and extending nearly to the Pacific Ocean?

The only fault of the Americans is that they will not rest satisfied with their success, but will always, in comparing themselves with European nations, claim superiority over them in everything. This is their great weakness, and encourages writers who come here to find fault.

I admire the American who remains American, but I cannot help feeling pity for one who considers Europe inferior to his new-born country.

XXXIII.

NEW YORK, August 2, 1840.

M. DE LA FOREST proposed yesterday that we should go on board the British Queen, which is still in the harbor, and bid Pageot good-by. I was foolish enough to accept. I had scarcely got on board this great vessel, which exactly resembles the Great Western, and on which I found three persons who came over with me and who were returning to Europe already, than I was overcome with such sad emotion, that I left as quickly as possible, and to-day I am still oppressed by a mortal sadness. I have positively what our French soldiers call "home-sickness."

Yesterday evening, wishing to raise my *spirits*, I called for M. de Menou, and we went to old Mr. Gallatin's, whom I was anxious to see, having heard M. de Talleyrand often speak of him. He received me very cordially; he is a handsome man of eighty years of age, and in full possession of all his mental faculties. You no doubt recollect his remarkable appearance, with strong, sharp-cut features, and an expression of great intelligence. He conversed with great ease about France, England, and the United States, about things of the past and present; a great deal also, and very well, of M. de Talleyrand.

I must say, in speaking of this conversation, that the only thing that attaches me to this country is the universal consideration accorded to M. de Talleyrand, whose memory is honored on every occasion, not only by those who have known him, but also by those who have heard him spoken of. It is not to flatter my sentiments that they speak thus in my presence, for here they never put themselves out for anything or any one. Mr. Gallatin said yesterday, with great truth, that one of the most remarkable traits in the character of M. de Talleyrand was that in the midst of all the different events of his life he always remained a good Frenchman, loving France before all and above all; and he told us in support of this eulogium a fact relating to Louisiana which took place during the residence of M. de Talleyrand in the United States, and consequently at a time when he was exiled and persecuted by his country.

XXXIV.

New York, August 7, 1840.

I KNOW now what a storm is in America; our storms in Europe can give one no idea of it. We had one yesterday which commenced at eleven o'clock in the morning and lasted until ten at night. The sound of the thunder is frightful, and the reverberation is succeeded by continual flashes of lightning, giving you no time to recover yourself! The lightning struck the steeple of a church, two buildings in the harbor, and one in an island near the city, killing two children. The heavy fall of rain undermined several houses.

I went a few days ago to Paterson, a charming place, where there are waterfalls and a manufactory of arms. I found M. Menou here, who took me to see his friend Mr. Colt, owner of almost the whole town, which contains five thousand inhabitants and thirty factories, placed on the waterfalls of the prettiest river in the world, which has retained its Indian name, *the Passaic River*. I prefer the Indian names to those which the Americans give to most of their towns, and which they have taken from the ancient and modern names of Europe, such as Rome, Carthage, Florence, Syracuse, Paris, Havre de Grâce: these with the Indian names form a ridiculous medley.

Mr. Colt took us first to the manufactory of arms, where carbines and pistols are made, which by a new and wonderful invention can be fired seven times in fifteen seconds, without reloading; he then took us to a factory of cotton cloth for sails, to another of paper, and to one where steam-engines were made. The situation is picturesque and charming; the ground is covered with weeping willows, which dip their branches in the *pretty* Passaic, and with catalpas and sycamores; trees of the same species which we see in Europe do not at all resemble the giant trees which grow in this country.

Mr. Colt, after introducing me to his wife and daughters and asking me to dinner, very kindly begged me to pay him a visit of several days.

M. Mollien, our Consul-General at Havana, is here and has just left me. He is a great traveller: he has visited the interior of Africa and the two Americas; he has lived in Havana during the last six years, and is so accustomed to the heat there, that here when we are broiling he complains of the cold. He spoke of the Countess Merlin, whom he saw when she sailed for Europe. Before leaving Havana, she gave a grand public concert in a hall larger than that of the Opera at Paris; she sang for the poor, and notwithstanding the exorbitant price of tickets, the hall was filled. Some went from curiosity, and others from duty; all the nobility of the country being related to her were obliged to go, and the receipts amounted to thirty thousand francs. But her singing was not liked; they did not go so far as to hiss her, but distinct murmurs of disapprobation were often heard. Her journey has been fortunate for her in other ways; she has obtained from her brothers a draft for two hundred thousand francs, and received between fifty and sixty thousand francs in presents from her family. It is an old custom in Havana to make presents to a young girl who is going to be married, or on any particular occasion—as for instance when about to make a long journey: all her relations, even the most distant, then give either presents of gold or of jewelry.

M. Mollien gives a very attractive description of Havana: it is the only colony that is prosperous at the present time. It is the most valuable jewel in the crown of Spain, and supplies the Queen with three hundred thousand francs a month for her pin-money. The inhabitants are rich and happy, and notwithstanding their wealth, which would allow of a great display of luxury, the life there is very simple. The heat prevents one from going out between the hours of eight in the morning and six in the evening, but in the houses, which are built of stone and arched, one does not suffer. They have terraces on the roof, where one can walk during the cool and charming nights. The inhabitants are divided into three classes: the Spaniards, who are not agreeable; the creoles, who are charming; and the negroes, who are treated with so much kindness that they form almost part of the family; they are gentle, obedient, and devoted even to fanaticism. It is just the reverse in the United States, where they have been brutalized and degraded by contempt and bad treatment, until they have become vulgar and depraved.

XXXV.

NEW YORK, August 11, 1840.

I DINED yesterday with Doctor Berger and his wife, his daughter fourteen years old, and three or four Frenchmen, the flower of the French colony, which is very numerous, but not very select. Fanny Elssler was the subject of conversation. Just imagine—at Baltimore the young men when she came out from the theatre detached the horses from her carriage and drew it themselves to her hotel! She comes to New York to-morrow, and they have made arrangements here for a grand serenade with one hundred and fifty German musicians, who are to play during the night under her windows, and will be escorted by the subscribers on horseback, carrying torches. The Americans think they prove by these acts of madness that they have as good taste as Europeans, and know how to appreciate talent.

I must tell you another characteristic trait, which will give you some idea of the people with whom I have the pleasure of living. Coming out of a restaurant where I had dined, I took a carriage from the stand—a sort of citadine with two wheels; I had my umbrella in my hand, and the coachman asked me to lend it to him. This I did willingly, at the same time noting the little specimen of democratic liberty.

Mr. Wickoff, the *beau* of Fanny Elssler, came yesterday to tell me that she wished to see me: I went, and found her having herself painted. She wanted me to say a good word for her to M. Mollien, whom she will meet in Havana, where she spends next winter. She will not return to Paris until spring. She has made eighty thousand francs in three months, and will certainly gain three times as much during her tour through the principal cities of the United States. There is a perfect furore for her here! The spectators act like mad-men when she dances.

She showed me a letter from the late King

of Prussia, written five months ago: in it he begs her to come to Berlin, that he may see her once more before he dies.

XXXVI.

<small>New York, August 15, 1840.</small>

I WENT yesterday to the Park Theatre to see Fanny in the ballet of the Tarentula and afterward in the Cracovienne. The beautiful Elssler, as the American newspapers call her, danced very well, but the rest of the ballet was pitiable: so truly grotesque, that it must have been a great annoyance to her.

In the evening, when the serenade by the Germans ought to have taken place, my valet, who wished to hear it, went under Elssler's window with the proprietor of our house; but the American people not liking the idea of the serenade, came with torches and drove the Germans away, and then burnt their music-stands and music. This is how they understand liberty in this strange country.

XXXVII.

New York, August 17, 1840.

YESTERDAY morning I had a visit from our Consul, M. de la Forest, who had just come from Philadelphia, where he had been to see his daughter, Madame d'Hauterive. I went with him to Hoboken, a village on a height opposite New York, where there is a hotel looked upon as a pleasure resort, and in which there are about thirty guests, with whom we dined. Among them I will mention a Mrs. Anderson, who is very pretty; she has lived in Paris two years, during which time her husband was the American Secretary of Legation. The other guests were French and American merchants staying there for a few weeks with their families; all very common people of course, but still less so than the same class of people would be in Europe.

After dinner M. de la Forest took me to a very pretty little house, a real English cottage in a nest of flowers, belonging to an American family, with whom two daughters of Madame F—— were staying. This grand niece of M.

de Sèze is the intimate friend of our Consul, and one of her daughters is engaged to be married to his son, who is Vice-Consul at Caracas. According to the father, his intimacy with the family is due to this engagement. According to the French colony, the engagement is due to the intimacy of the parents. It has given occasion to great scandal, to caricatures and newspaper articles; it is certain that Madame de la Forest, who has been in France during the last three years, opposes as strongly as she can the marriage of her son with Mademoiselle F——. However, we took these two young ladies, who are decidedly ugly, in our carriage, and drove twelve miles through the most beautiful country—partly along the shores of the North River, and partly on those of a little river called the *Hackewai*.*

The young girls here so celebrated for their beauty have not a healthy look; their manners are not pleasant; they are cold-blooded coquettes; they tantalize the men, and while not concealing their desire to find a husband, they do not seem to care to find in him anything else than a companion. As to the

---

* Apparently the Hackensack.

women, they are all faded, worn out, finished, after two years of marriage. The lady to whom the cottage we saw yesterday belongs who it seems was lovely at twenty years of age, is now at twenty-six a frightful ruin—nothing but skin and bone, and with a very coarse complexion.

We received news from London to the 3d by the steamer Acadia, which made the voyage to Halifax in twelve days, and from there to New York in thirty-six hours. This is a very short time to travel twelve hundred leagues, but very long to one so far away from his country.

War between France and England is the topic of conversation everywhere, and the subject of discussion in every newspaper. Without exactly blaming us, they laugh at the bragging articles in our papers, which, they say, never come to anything, and only throw ridicule on the French Government. They add that if we really go to war it will be for something of very little consequence, and as usual for glory, without any profit to us. The Americans are matter-of-fact people, attracted by the substance and not the shadow. And I have already seen that they do not think much of us; notwithstanding their complimentary speeches, they do not feel the slightest gratitude for the aid given them by France in their War of Independence; and the indemnity of twenty-five millions paid five years ago has finished us in their opinion. They see that we can always be duped. It is a singular fact that they fear the English, whose writers never cease to ridicule them, and yet their tastes and inclinations are English. It is true they have the same origin, the same manners, customs, and religion; but the Revolution of 1776, the Peace of 1783, and the War of 1812 ought, it would seem, to have put an insurmountable barrier between these two nations, and, above all, when one thinks of the contempt with which the English treat the Americans. Well, the Americans admire and imitate *John Bull*. As soon as they have a little money, they want a house in the English style. Then it is only in England and Scotland that an American can satisfy his pride of birth. The first thing he does after he has made a fortune is to seek in England proofs of his descent from some English family, and on his return to have the coat of arms of this family engraved on his silver. There are many contradictions in this Nation, which is still in its infancy and in a transition state.

I have read again with great care M. de Tocqueville's work, "Democracy in America." The two last volumes are not equal to the first ones. In these there is a general exposure, which is clear and exact, of the weak errors in the construction of the Constitution of the United States, whether federal or particular to each of the States of the federation. There is also a faithful picture of the American character at the time, for this character is constantly modified by a thousand causes too many to enumerate: it is sufficient to speak of immigration, which throws one hundred thousand Europeans on the American continent every year. Thus I recognize as true the picture which M. de Tocqueville gives of the *Yankee* of New England, and also of the Southerner, of the Virginian and Georgian, proprietors of slaves, and living in the midst of the slavery of the blacks. But one sees plainly in the last two volumes of his work, published five years after his departure from the United States, that the object of the author is, while giving his ideas on the democracy of America, more or less new, and his reflections, which are mostly old, to apply them to the moral and political state of France. What in my opinion spoils M. de Tocqueville's work and partly takes away from the importance he wished to give it, is the comparison he tries to establish between the democracy of the United States and that of France. This comparison appears to me entirely imaginary; the fundamental points essential to it are wanting, or differ absolutely. We know that in the United States they owe the beginning of their organization to religious persecution, which drove the English and Scotch Puritans to the American Continent; that these men in establishing themselves there took for the principles upon which they founded their institutions the doctrines of the Gospel as interpreted by themselves. This is the explanation of the actual American Constitution, modified perhaps by the peculiar character of the Anglo-Americans, perhaps by the provincial and municipal institutions which the puritans brought with them from the mother-country. Taking this thread for a guide in the examination of the American Constitution, one can easily trace it to the present time. You see the gradual changes brought about by the increase of population; the desire to throw off the yoke of the mother Church; the Revolution of 1776, which was the result; the efforts of distinguished men who vainly sought to control this revolution or lessen the evil consequences; and later the Irish, German, and French emigration; the opening and civilizing of the West; the large private fortunes acquired by the creation of banks; then the ruin of these banks: and you come to understand the moral and political position of the United States at the present time. One may write volumes and comment forever on these events, but he must always return to this conclusion—that the mission to people and to civilize the American continent is intrusted by Providence to the Anglo-American race. It is a fact apart from history, and of which one can draw no conclusion from the rest of the world, that the consequences may be but transient and apply only to this fact, and that it is not improbable that as the United States becomes more thickly inhabited and civilized they will enter the common path by which other nations have passed, only retaining those particular traits belonging to each of them, such as cause a Russian to be distinguished from an Englishman, a Spaniard from a German.

But how can any one compare such a state of things to that of France? To France, the most ancient monarchy of Europe, which after having passed through a feudal government, and that of the brilliant despotism of Louis XIV. and the degrading despotism of Louis XV., extended to 1789, when the radical reform of her constitution inclined her to revolution. This revolution destroyed everything—institutions, morals, and religion; it upset the rights of property, but did it modify the national character as much as was supposed? This passion for equality, which it developed to such a degree—was it not more a desire to crush the higher classes and put themselves in their places, than a rational determination to equalize the condition of men? Have not the French always the same inclination to distinguish themselves, the same thirst for military glory? And this inclination for distinction, this thirst for military glory is nothing else but the desire of superiority applied to one's self, and of a personal aristocratic feeling. Every one has the desire to place himself above his equals: this is the secret of revolutions. That of 1789, in wishing to destroy everything, could not blot out the history of the last eighteen centuries; it could not prevent memories of the past and traditions being perpetuated; it could not prevent France, surrounded by other countries where aristocratic sentiments were still honored, finding points of comparison every day, which, if they excited the hatred of some, kept up the ambition of others.

To sum up: I say that the democracy, which they tell us is final, appears to me to be in a state of transition, and that in any case that which exists in the United States cannot be compared to that of France. American democracy is approaching the boundary-lines of aristocracy, and perhaps toward a limited monarchy. French democracy is going I don't know where, but I think more toward despotism than toward a republic. Whatever they do, absolute equality of condition is a dream which cannot be realized. It is contrary to the nature of things and contrary to human nature. The rich man is an aristocrat in the eyes of the poor, the savant in those of the ignorant, the strong man in those of the feeble; and I do not know of any system of equality possible except it be in a nation composed of citizens who are poor, weak, and ignorant to the same degree, and this would not be a nation, but an assemblage, an agglomeration of slaves, who would soon become a prey to their neighbors.

XXXVIII.

NEW YORK, August 23, 1840.

HAVING established my head-quarters here during the very warm weather, I have accepted an invitation to the club, that I may quietly study the character of the people with whom I am condemned to live; besides which, I can dine there more at my ease than elsewhere.

I went yesterday with M. Menou to the extreme end of New York, to a quarter which ought to be the most elegant in the city; but the buildings there have been left unfinished in consequence of the financial crisis, which has now lasted four years. It is curious to see these unfinished buildings: it looks as if the work had been stopped by the enchanted ring of some evil spirit. These buildings, when finished, will be larger but not handsomer than those of other parts of the town: they are of the same very red brick, the same very green shutters, the same very white doors—altogether hideous. The University, of Gothic architecture, and Washington Square are a little better than the rest. And, what a beautiful place this city could be made, situated between two rivers which can be seen on the right and left from the end of each street! The situation is admirable; there is no place that can compare with it; and not a curiosity to see, and not an edifice you can speak of.

I met Baron Mareschall yesterday on the Battery, with Count Colombiano, chargé d'affaires of Sardinia, one of my colleagues, whose acquaintance I had not yet made; he is, like me, an invalid, and lives in Washington only when obliged to; he seemed agreeable and well-bred. While continuing our walk we watched the rising of a magnificent storm.

The sky grew dark and the harbor was entirely obscured, except when lit up occasionally by flashes of lightning—more like volcanic eruptions than our poor little flashes in Europe. We went home in the midst of formidable claps of American thunder, hoping the storm would cool the air for to-day; but it has not done anything of the kind, and last night I had my first experience of mosquitoes, who become gay and festive only during the hottest weather; they never left me quiet for a moment.

I have seen the superb steamer called the President; her deck is three hundred feet long, but her interior accommodations are not nearly as good as those of the Great Western. If I return to Europe I shall most certainly do so on an English ship. The American and French ships are uncomfortable and unsafe, owing to the rapacity of the one and negligence of the other. I have seen something here which is very curious: it is an artist who takes portraits by daguerrotype; they are frightful pictures, and only give the features without any expression or shades; they are like the skeleton of a face, black and hideous;

but this reproduction fixed on glass is nevertheless a very strange invention, and if it should be perfected, will be very useful. These likenesses, which would be such consolation in absence, will be within the reach of persons with small purses. M. Mollien and I had ourselves *drawn*. This is the expression in use. We were frightful, and appeared at least a hundred years old; the operation lasted scarcely five minutes.

XXXIX.

NEW YORK, August 29, 1840.

I WENT yesterday morning with M. de la Forest to *Roccaway*, the most fashionable place for sea-bathing in the country. We crossed the East River in a ferryboat, and landed at Brooklyn City, one of those towns which have been laid out, and in which very few houses have as yet been built, all work having been stopped on account of the disastrous financial situation. Brooklyn is opposite New York, on Long Island; taking the railroad there, we arrived, in one hour's journey, across a beautiful, well-wooded country, at a lovely village, *Jamaisa*, destined soon to become a city The railroad is only finished to this place, and we were obliged to ride eight miles farther in a miserable *char-a-bancs*, through a wild marshy country, before reaching the Pavilion of *Roccaway*.

This Pavilion, which is on the seashore, contains accommodation for one hundred persons. The beach is bare, gloomy, and monotonous—not a tree or a shrub; the arrangements for bathing are bad, and the bathing-houses unfit for use; and this is a sample of the watering-places they boast so much of! I was obliged to make a great many new acquaintances; among others, that of Madame Cigogne, whose ridiculous name I have already spoken of, and of her daughter Mademoiselle Adèle Cigogne; they are creoles of Saint-Domingo, and emigrated to the United States when that island was in a state of rebellion. They established a boarding-school for young girls at Philadelphia, as I think I told you. Mademoiselle Cigogne is about fifty years old and still very handsome, with perfectly regular features, and the expressive countenance of the creole. She has also a great deal of intelligence and wit. These ladies invited me to visit them in Philadelphia, which I shall certainly do with the greatest pleasure, this splendid old maid being one of the most agreeable women I have ever met.

The Count de Grasse was presented to me by his own request, although he is a Legitimist. He is the son of Admiral de Grasse; his sister married a M. de Pau, whose daughter is Madame Mortimer Livingston, and whose son is married to Miss Thorn. I also made the acquaintance of Mr. and Mrs. Mortimer Livingston, who is *distinguée* and melancholy, and of Mrs. Davis of Philadelphia: she is frightfully ugly, but intelligent, and an artist.

I have at last seen Madame Jerome Bonaparte,—Miss Patterson,—a large fat woman, whose face still preserves traces of wonderful beauty, but totally devoid of expression; she looks like a plaster model in a studio enlarged. They say she is an agreeable woman, but I pronounce her dreadfully tedious. She has just come from Paris, and talked to me of the Pontécoulants as her intimate friends.

At two o'clock we sat down, one hundred and twenty, at table. After dinner the women played ten-pins under a shed closed in on three sides. There I saw the most singular spectacle. The *gentlemen* took off their coats and vests, lit their cigars, joined in the game with these ladies, who did not seem in the least shocked. A young lady, said to be one of the greatest beauties in New York, and celebrated as an amateur singer, made herself very conspicuous by her free behavior and manners with the *gentlemen* in their shirt-sleeves. I cannot get accustomed to these things.

Fanny Elssler has given her last performance in New York; it was her benefit. She made a little *speach* in English at the close of the performance, which had a prodigious success. No conqueror after a victory was ever applauded as she was.

XL.

New York, September 2, 1840.

I STARTED at seven o'clock yesterday morning to pay Mr. Hamilton a visit at Newis. He met me at the steamboat landing, and took me to his house, which is on a height; we arrived there at ten o'clock. It is a pretty dwelling, arranged and furnished in English fashion, but built of wood, which must make it difficult to keep warm in bad weather. The view is enchanting: it takes in thirty miles of the Hudson, a magnificent river, which opposite Newis is three miles broad; perpendicular rocks which are called the Palisades extend eight miles along the opposite shore. The Hudson is covered with boats of all kinds—steamboats, and boats with white sails; the horizon is shut out on both sides by lovely hills, covered with trees, and cottages in every direction surrounded with flowers. The Hudson is often compared with the Rhine; but is far superior in size and grandeur, the Rhine is richer in traditions, and must rest content in the pride of its feudal ruins.

Mr. Hamilton presented me to his wife and four daughters: the eldest, Mrs. Shuyler, is ugly; she speaks French very well; the second, Mrs. Bowdwins, stared at me all the time, and didn't say a word in any language; the third, Miss Mary, was equally silent; the fourth, Miss Angelique, is very pretty and lively. Taking them altogether, including little Alexander, whom you know, and who was not there, they are an agreeable family; they overwhelmed me with polite attentions, and I shall be delighted to see them again in Washington, where they propose passing two months next winter.

After the morning tea, Mr. Hamilton took me to see the Mesdames Jones, his neighbors, who took us to see Mr. Washington Irving, whose place adjoins theirs. Mr. Hamilton wished to ask him to dine with me, but he had just left for New York. Mr. Irving is not married, and lives with his four nieces, who received us; not one of them is pretty, but their faces and manners are agreeable. The house is lovely: it is Holland House in miniature—climbing plants outside, books and comfort inside. We walked back to Newis through the woods, by a path overhanging the Hudson. I forgot to tell you that Washington Irving's reputation as a literary man stands highest in America; I should have been glad to have seen him. At two o'clock we had a good dinner and well served, and at four I left Newis and my kind hosts.

XLI.

Boston, September 5, 1840.

I LEFT New York the day before yesterday, at six o'clock in the morning with M. de la Forest and two of Madame F——'s daughters: one is the future daughter-in-law of our Consul, and the other is also to be married soon. The steamboat took us up the East River to New Haven, where we arrived at one o'clock; we then took the railroad and arrived in two hours at Hartford, where we stayed all night. After dinner we walked through the town. There is an oak-tree here which they say is five hundred years old: it is hollow, and two hundred years ago, a charter given by the King of England, and which he afterward wished to

withdraw, was hidden in it. This tree is called
the Charter Oak. I took an acorn away with
me. Hartford is one of the learned cities of
the United States; her university is celebrated;
there is another at New Haven, also in great
repute; the third is in Cambridge, one mile from
Boston. The oldest inhabited States pay most
attention to the sciences. New Haven and
Hartford are the two capitals of Connecticut,
one of the richest and most advanced States
in New England; the Legislature of the State
meets alternately at one or the other city.

We visited an insane asylum, which was admirably kept; a crazy woman asked me where
I came from; when I told her that I came from
New York, she said with a melancholy voice,
"*I know it, but I am forever out of the world.*"
The physician said, however, that she was getting well.

We left Hartford at eight in the morning by
the stage. It was the first time I had travelled
by one in America—they are not much better
than those in France; the country through
which we passed is lovely, and would recall
England if more thickly settled. After having
passed through places called Berlin, Windsor,

Grafton, and Newton, without stopping, we arrived at Springfield, where we dined, and then travelled ninety miles in five hours, on a splendid railroad and through a beautiful cultivated country. A lovely sunset added to our enjoyment of a splendid view of Boston. The city is built in the form of an amphitheatre around the shores of the ocean; it contains one hundred and twenty thousand inhabitants, including four or five towns in the suburbs— *Broaklin, Cambridge, Charlestown, etc.* Boston is the oldest town in the United States, built two hundred years ago, and the streets are narrower and the houses higher than in more recently built towns; it is a beautiful English town.

M. Isnard, the French Consul, who had been advised of my coming, had fortunately secured rooms for me; otherwise it would have been difficult, as there was a political meeting of the opponents of Mr. Van Buren to be held on the 10th of this month, which will draw about sixty thousand strangers here. Fanny Elssler and the indispensable Wickoff are staying in the same hotel with us: I am fated to meet them everywhere.

XLII.

BOSTON, September 6, 1840.

IT has rained all day. The little F——s have been reading and working from early this morning till night. They have been well brought up, and *not too much troublesome*. M. de la Forest and I have been to see Mademoiselle Elssler, who was very anxious about her first performance, which takes place tomorrow. It appears that the musicians and ballet are not ready, and would not rehearse either last night or during to-day, on account of their puritanic notions of keeping Sunday.

I have taken advantage of a brightening of the sky to go to see the State House, a large building in which the Senate and Representatives of the State of Massachusetts, of which Boston is the capital, meet. From the cupola of this building there is a beautiful panorama of Boston and its environs. The town is situated on a peninsula, surrounded by the sea and connected by bridges with different parts of the mainland, where there are several small towns: South Boston, containing manufactories and public establishments; Cambridge, where *Howard College* is—the most celebrated university in the United States, with six hundred students; Charlestown, in which are the State Prison, the Insane Hospital, the *Navy gard*, and *Bunker Hills*, a monument built in memory of a victory over the English on June 17, 1776. There are in Boston a great many stores, depots, and shops; docks, where innumerable vessels come from all parts of the world; and four railroads. There is a beautiful public walk in the centre of the town, well laid out with trees, and near it the commencement of a botanical garden. They have difficulty in keeping the sea from encroaching on it. The houses surrounding the public grounds are built of granite, and in many streets the *area* are filled with flowers; and, to complete the charm of this city, there are no hogs to be seen wandering about the streets, as in other cities of the United States. There is no doubt that altogether things are better here than in other places. Society is composed of a sort of financial aristocracy, well brought up, religious, and honest. There are fifty-two churches in the city and suburbs, of which four are Catholic. The market is clean and luxurious, a quarter of a mile in length, well heated, and lit with gas. The market-women are dressed with an approach to elegance.

XLIII.

BOSTON, September 7, 1840.

THE weather has changed from extreme heat to freezing. We saw *Mount Auburn Cimetery* yesterday; it reminds one of Père-Lachaise. This cemetery is embellished by superb trees and lovely avenues; these bear the names of the trees with which they are planted—*Cedar Avenue*, *Poplar Avenue*, *Azelea Avenue*. The tombs are on the right and left, placed like houses on a street. I remarked that of Spurzheim, the disciple of Gall, who died in Boston in 1832.

On quitting the cemetery we went to Fresh Pond, which is like the Pool of Saint-Gratien, in the valley of Montmorency. From there to the University, which is called *Howard College*,[*] a *Mr. Howard* having been the founder.

---

[*] Obviously Harvard College.

Almost all the public institutions here are indebted to private individuals of wealth for their foundation; it is an honorable trait in the *Yankee* character, but not exempt from ostentation. The University occupies a large extent of ground. The buildings are handsome and the gardens charming.

We then went to Charlestown, where the monument of *Bunker's Hise* is being built, on the spot where, at the commencement of the War for Independence, three hundred Americans defended themselves against ten thousand English. This monument is to be a simple obelisk of granite in the middle of a grass-plat, from which there is a beautiful view. For want of funds the obelisk has only reached to one third of its intended height, but a meeting of American ladies has been called to propose means for its completion. Near by is the convent of the Benedictines, which was broken into, pillaged, and burnt by the Bostonians three years ago, from pure curiosity to see what was going on there, incited by the most absurd stories. The Bishop of Boston, in consequence of this, sent the nuns to their principal house in Canada.

Afterward he claimed damages from the City of Boston and from the Legislature of Massachusetts. On their refusal he declared that he would leave the ruins just as they were. As the ground belongs to the Catholic Church, he had the right to do as he pleased, and this determination annoys the Protestants very much, because all strangers view these ruins with astonishment and ask the cause.

After dinner I took a walk through the streets, which, on account of its being Sunday, were almost deserted; however, the chains which formerly closed all the streets to prevent carriages from passing during Sunday, were only drawn around the churches. Boston is perfectly clean. No one is allowed to put any dirt on the public highways; they keep it all in the interior of their houses, and the city authorities have it carried away every morning at the expense of the city. There is a fine of twenty-five francs for smoking in the streets.

XLIV.

Boston, September 10, 1840.

The only fault of Boston in my eyes—but it is a great one—is that the inhabitants of this elegant and charming city hate the French, and what is worse, they despise them. They have retained the inveterate English prejudices of two centuries ago against France, and this would make my stay here for any length of time insupportable.

We went to Salem, a pretty little seaport town near which the first Pilgrims landed in the time of Charles I. The whole coast is rocky. There is a maritime museum here, founded forty years ago, by a club whose members must prove that they have doubled Cape Horn and the Cape of Good Hope; consequently they are almost all captains of vessels. They are bound to bring some object of antiquity on their return from every voyage, and deposit it in the museum, which has been filled in this way.

The Boston ladies hold a fair to-day, the proceeds of which are to go toward the completion of the monument of *Bunker's Hise*. A gentleman presented to this fair a snuff-box which he pretends to have bought at a sale of Prince Talleyrand's effects in Paris. It is a worthless box, which has seen much service, and has a corner broken off. It is proposed to buy it, and present it to a Major Russell, who is eighty-four years old, and is said to have been very intimate with M. de Talleyrand. I did not wish to destroy the value of this box by telling them that M. de Talleyrand never took snuff.

XLV.

NEW YORK, September 11, 1840.

WE went by rail yesterday to Providence, where we arrived at noon. This is the capital of the little State of Rhode Island. It is a town of twenty thousand inhabitants, beautifully situated on the Providence River, thirty-five miles from the sea. At six o'clock we were in Stonington, a pretty port on the ocean. We took the steamer, and at eight o'clock in the morning arrived at New York.

At noon we went on an excursion up the Hudson River. After having visited *Barnham House* and *Stiker's Boy*, we arrived at *Monalton City*,* then at *Macomb's Dam*, on the East River, and there we saw the Croton Aqueduct, which is being built to bring good drinking-water to New York, where now there is not a drop. This aqueduct will be twenty-eight leagues in length, and will not be finished for three or four years.

On my return to New York I went to see a diorama exhibited by some Frenchmen who had asked my patronage.

XLVI.

New York, September 14, 1840.

I WENT this morning to see the grounds, six miles from town, on which preparations are being made for a new cemetery. It will be like a magnificent English park. The Americans take great care of their dead; when I remarked this as greatly to their praise, some one said it was not a question of sentiment, but of self-love. On the highest point of this

---

* Apparently Manhattanville.

cemetery, which will be called "*Greenwood Cimetery*," there is a level piece of ground, on which it is proposed to erect a monument in memory of General Washington. The view from this point is certainly the most beautiful in the whole world.

I went afterward on board the North Carolina, an American man-of-war and school for young midshipmen; I was requested in Paris to obtain information about this school. I have examined into the subject thoroughly.

I have also visited the *penitentiary;* the situation is so charming that it has been named *Mount pleasant's Penitentiary.* It is a kind of fortress on an island in the East River; there are three hundred men and four hundred and fifty women there, who are made to work, but not much; it is more like a house of improvement than of correction. Sixteen keepers are sufficient to keep these seven or eight hundred prisoners in order. The man who acted as my guide, a true American, gave it as his opinion that it would require a regiment of the line to restrain so many prisoners in our country. He said that most of them were Germans, and was very much confused to find that not one of those to whom I spoke their supposed language could understand me, but answered in English, saying they were Americans. My conductor confided to me that the women were much more difficult to manage than the men; they tried their powers of fascination on the jailers. The stamp of crime was more pronounced on the faces of these wretches than in Europe. Doctor Bénit, who came with me, examined them from the phrenological point of view with great interest.

XLVII.

PHILADELPHIA, September 24, 1840.

WE left New York on the 19th, on a large steamboat, which carried us to South Amboy, where we took the railroad, which brought us to Bordentown on the Delaware. In this pretty little town are the house and grounds of Joseph Bonaparte. The steamboat took us down the Delaware River to Philadelphia, passing Bristol in Pennsylvania and Burlington in New Jersey.

I dined the day after my arrival with our Consul, M. d'Hauterive; there was no one but his wife, and a Doctor Laroche, a creole of Saint-Domingo and nephew of Madame Cigogne. Madame d'Hauterive seems to be a mild, good little woman. Brought up at the Sacred Heart in Paris, she talked of nothing but Monsignor de Quélen, Madame de Gramont, and Madame Marbœuf. After dinner we all went to Madame Cigogne's, whose house is elegant and the society select; it is very curious to see a mistress of a boarding-school in such a position. The whole evening was passed in relating amusing anecdotes of the Quakers. These ladies are not at all prudish.

I have seen the Exchange, which is curiously arranged; there is a large hall, where are newspapers from all parts of the world. The whole appearance is more elegant than at New York.

I went with M. d'Hauterive to see a dam which has been constructed on the river *Shuylkill*, about three miles from the town, from which the water is raised into reservoirs by an admirable machine; from there it is taken in pipes to Philadelphia and into each house. It is a superb work, executed on a grand scale.

We then went to Girard College, which is not far off. Girard was a workman of Bordeaux; he made an immense fortune here, and left by his will thirty million francs for the improvement of the city of Philadelphia. He drew the plan of this college himself, which is to be built entirely of white marble, and prescribed all the details, with penalty of forfeiture of the bequest if not strictly conformed to.

We went the same day to *Laurel Hill Cimetery*, the appearance of which is not at all gloomy or severe; it is more like a garden laid out for public amusements than a cemetery.

I went through the Philadelphia shops today; they are as well supplied as those of London and Paris. I saw some magnificent antique porcelain from China.

I was introduced to two old men, who interested me very much—M. du Ponceau, eighty-four years old, blind and deaf, but who related the most amusing anecdotes with infinite wit and humor; and Mr. Vaughan, a little man of eighty years of age, who thinks himself but forty, and it is said makes the ladies think so too. " Full of life and gallantry!"

I visited the Blind Asylum. It is conducted on the French and German plan, and is perfectly managed. The director, thinking to do me a great honor, made the pupils play the Marseillaise on my entrance to the hall; they played so well that I really enjoyed it. There is a young man there who had been brought up in Paris, and who had asked to be received as a guest. He came to the United States eight years ago to make his fortune, and he did it, blind as he was; he worked in a commercial establishment on the Mississippi, and is here now on their business. This poor young man interested me very strongly, and also amused me very much by relating his efforts to persuade the director not to have the Marseillaise played.

Doctor Bénit is in ecstasies since our visit to the *Pensylvania Hospital* founded by Penn. They receive there, in three separate buildings, the wounded, the women about to be confined, and the lunatics. Every particular is attended to in a manner unknown in Europe: the beds are perfect, the costumes of the patients are elegant, and the linen very fine; there are carpets on all the rooms, and even on the stairs. The air is changed constantly, and scented with sweet and agreeable perfumes. One could lodge there with comfort and pleasure. I found amongst the lunatics a Frenchman, Captain Poirier, Chevalier de Saint-Louis, and officer of the Legion of Honor. He had served in the Thirty-fifth of the line, in which my brother formerly served; when I mentioned this to him he recollected him perfectly well, and talked with me very reasonably for a quarter of an hour. He had been, under the Restoration, suspected of having connections with conspirators, and was put on half-pay. He then came to a free country that he might grumble at his ease against his own. Always posing as a victim, he kept himself in a constant state of excitement—so much so that he lost his mind, and the French Consul was obliged to have him shut up in this asylum, where the French Government has paid his board for seven years.

XLVIII.

Philadelphia, September 26, 1840.

The day before yesterday I rose very early that I might see the superb market in High Street, which is a mile in length, at its busiest time: it is covered and arranged in the most convenient manner; almost all the fruits and vegetables we see in Europe are there, with those of America. The peaches are enormous, but not so good as ours; in their gardens which are not carefully cultivated, everything is abundant and cheap. There were more men than women buying their provisions. In the United States, good housekeepers of the middle classes stay at home as much as possible, and do not trust their helps,—it is thus they call their servants,—to spend the money for household expenses; so you see perfectly well-dressed men carrying vegetables in a handkerchief in one hand and a leg of mutton in the other.

I have breakfasted with my two amiable old men: they talked of past times, of the American wars in which both had taken an active part. Old Vaughan had been the Secretary of Legation of Franklin, and was presented to Queen Marie Antoinette; the ladies of Versailles cried out in astonishment, "Oh! they are dressed like Frenchmen." No doubt they expected to see Hurons. They showed me the Athenæum Library where they spend most of their time, and have promised to give me a letter of Franklin's and one of Penn's, the founder of Pensylvania and of Philadelphia.

I have seen the tomb of Franklin in an old burying-ground; on a tombstone lying flat on the ground are simply cut these words:

"Benjamin and Deborah Franklin, 1790." Husband and wife died the same year.

The Chinese Museum in Philadelphia is the most curious thing of the kind that ever existed: it is composed of groups of Chinese of life size and so well made that one would take them for living beings; the costumes and the attitude are truly striking, and everything about them, the furniture and articles which they manufacture, are so arranged as to represent the interior of a Chinese home.

I went yesterday, accompanied as usual by

Doctor Benit, to see the Alms-house, a refuge for beggars, which has cost five millions to establish, and seven or eight hundred thousand a year to maintain, for the board and lodging of fifteen hundred paupers, who find themselves as well off as if each had ten thousand francs income. And yet almost all these people have been brought there by their misconduct and intemperance and have a most degraded look; but a government founded on equality cannot pay too dear for the luxury with which it surrounds these old libertines.

From this splendid edifice we went to the "Naval Hospital," on the left bank of the *Shuylkill*. The secretary of the house, who was kind enough to take us all through it, explained the uselessness of it; this establishment, which ought to be the "Hôtel des Invalides" of all the marine of the United States, as it belongs to the Federal Government, can accommodate two hundred veterans, but there are only about twenty here, the old sailors prefer to drink and live in poverty rather than have every comfort and be obliged to live governed by fixed rules. In this Hospital the money has been thrown away, and the whole plan has been badly carried out. Louis XIV., at the Invalides and England at Greenwich have done much better.

XLIX.

PHILADELPHIA, September 28, 1840.

MR. VAUGHAN came to see me yesterday, and told me all kinds of anecdotes of M. de Talleyrand, M. de Liancourt, M. de Beaumetz, M. de Noailles, and King Louis Philippe, whom he saw every evening at Mr. Bingham's, Lady Ashburton's father. Mr. Vaughan's brother received M. de Talleyrand's letters in London and sent them to him in America. Vaughan told me of several speculations which M. de Talleyrand had wished to make in the United States, and which had great promise of success. He took me to the Franklin Institute, where they have lectures on mechanics every day; any one may attend, and even workmen may receive instruction there by paying a very small annual contribution.

We then went to the State Penitentiary, a famous institution, where *the solitary confine-*

ment has been established for the first time. Messrs. De Tocqueville and De Beaumont describe it minutely in their work on the Penitentiary system; they took up their abode there for fifteen days. It is a fortress like that of Vincennes, of an *amful* aspect. I was shown everything in detail and allowed to talk freely to the prisoners, who are condemned to perfect silence. Each one I talked to declared he was innocent.

I have also seen *the home of refuge for juvenile delinquents*. They reform boys and girls under eighteen years old with great success.

In the evening I went to Madame Cigogne's, where I found about a dozen persons: they said that when King Louis Philippe was in Philadelphia he was very attentive to a Miss Perkins, who resembled very much our Queen Amélie.

Mr. Toland took me this morning to see the Mansion House, which was formerly the residence of Mr. Bingham, and is now a hotel. He then took me to the end of a blind alley, and showed me a miserable-looking house occupied by a German baker named Brescht.

M. de Talleyrand lived in this house during his stay in Philadelphia.

Last night I went to the Athenæum Library; this is Mr. Vaughan's reception-room. He brings people here every Friday to converse, and during the winter to play whist. I met old Du Ponceau here, who related a thousand silly things about M. de Talleyrand which he got from Joseph Bonaparte, who was only too glad to put any of his brother the Grand Emperor's follies on him. Luckily I knew all about it, and was able to give the true story.

At the Athenæum I made the acquaintance of *Mr. Bidole*, whose name as a financier has been so well known. As President of the Bank of the United States he struggled for several years against General *Jakson*.

I intended leaving to-morrow, but De la Forest and D'Hauterive have so urgently begged me to remain for the Grand Mass of Haydn, in which Madame d'Hauterive sings, that out of politeness I have decided to stay.

L.

BALTIMORE, September 30, 1840.

THE Grand Mass, with the music of Madame d'Hauterive and company, lasted nearly four hours, thanks to a Jesuit who delivered a sermon of an hour and a half in honor of Saint Ignatius of Loyola. It was the birthday of this Saint, whose whole history he told us without pity; he then spoke of the misfortunes, successes, and prosperity of the Jesuits. I learned that in olden times they numbered thirty thousand! What an army! there are only one tenth of them left now.

I left Philadelphia yesterday at eight o'clock in the morning by the "Susquehanna Railroad." Four miles from Philadelphia there is an inclined plane rising one hundred and fifty-seven feet, up which the cars are drawn by ropes with pulleys; travellers prefer generally to walk up, just as they do when travelling in diligences. The descent is into a charming valley, through which we travelled seventy miles to Columbia, where I slept. This valley, or rather plain, which is immense, is the richest and most beautiful part of Pennsylvania; it is undulating, wooded, and cultivated. There are no towns or villages on the road, but only scattered dwellings, most beautifully located. All this country has been peopled and cultivated by Germans; some even to the third generation still talk in German. *Lanscaster,* which we passed through, is a very short distance from *Colombia,* and is inhabited entirely by Germans.

After leaving Colombia this morning I saw a range of mountains, the commencement of the *Alleghanys,* which separate the Atlantic States from the Western. We crossed the *Susquehana* on a wooden covered bridge one mile and a half long. This bridge does great credit to the American engineer who built it. We passed near the city of York, and went through a different country from that we travelled yesterday, but equally pretty of its kind; the most picturesque woods, fields, rocks, and streams, with a most glorious sun gilding the leaves just beginning to turn yellow. While enjoying this charming view we arrived in Baltimore.

LI.

WASHINGTON, October 5, 1840.

I HAVE just paid my first visit to Mr. Forsyth, who is sick, nervous, and irritable. The prospects of the coming election are not favorable to the present Administration, and increase his irritability; he is a man of intelligence, but one who affects never to speak seriously. He is always trying to entrap one in conversation, and turn everything into ridicule; he is both tiresome and disagreeable.

I also went to see the President, Mr. Van Buren, who is living at a country place four miles from here. He is also suffering and uneasy: I am sorry that his chances for re-election are so bad; it would be better to retain him than risk an unknown person. Besides, I think he is very well disposed toward France, and is very courteous to me. His politeness is perfect: it is the perfect imitation of a *gentleman*.

LII.

WASHINGTON, October 10, 1840.

ON the 6th, M. de Lafosse, M. Montholon, and I left here for Alexandria at nine o'clock in the morning; we dined there and after a two hours' ride over the most abominable road arrived at the entrance to Mount Vernon Park; we crossed this park, which is very badly kept, on foot. At first we were refused entrance to the house. I sent in my card, and we were immediately received by Mrs. Washington, widow of General Washington's nephew. This lady was very polite, and immediately offered us refreshments, which we did not accept. She then showed us a key of the Bastille and a picture of it taken at the time of its destruction; these were sent to General Washington by General Lafayette. She also showed us a bust of General Lafayette presented by him, and one of General Washington, the cast for which was taken from his body after death; an engraving of Louis XVI.; the library of General Washington, and the Bible he was in the habit of reading. These are the curiosities and relics which are in her possession. She then gave us in charge of a dirty oily negress to take us to see the tomb of the General, which is at the end of the garden in a low place. It is a vault built of brick, before which is an arch protected by iron railings; under this arch are two tombs in white marble; on one is the name of the General surmounted by his arms; on the other the name of his wife. An inscription on one side of the tomb of the General indicates that this sarcophagus was presented to the family of the deceased by a marble-cutter of Philadelphia. All this is as *shabby* as possible: the park is overgrown with weeds, the tomb is ugly and mean-looking, the house tumbling down; everything dirty and in a miserable condition; and the appearance of Mrs. Washington is pitiable. The country ought to do something for a place which gratitude should make sacred in their eyes, and for a family whose evident poverty is a stigma on the United States. Mount Vernon is beautifully situated on the banks of the Potomac; the house overlooks the country, and opposite is Fort Washington, which is very imposing. It would cost very little to give this resting-place of General Washington the dignity which is due to it. He was the greatest man of the country, and the only brilliant point in American history. The United States owe their existence and prosperity to his genius, and he lies forgotten amidst uncultivated bushes, and near his house, which will soon be in ruins!

I will now give you a perfectly true history, which is very little known, and very dishonorable to the English. After the fatal peace of 1753, by which France ceded a great part of Canada, and with it Acadia, to England, the English Government began by changing the name Acadia to Nova Scotia, which name it still bears; then in 1755 they published an order, that all the inhabitants without exception should go on September 5 to certain places in different parts of the country. They went there, not suspecting the purpose for which they were sent, and to avoid the punishment with which they were threatened if they failed to obey. The different gatherings were then informed that by a decree of the British Government all their property of whatever kind was confiscated to the Crown of England; that they would be allowed to take with them only their ready money and clothes, and must quit the country, and be transported into the farthest point in Canada. The day for their departure—that is to say, five days after the publication of September 10—the troops were ordered out to force those who were unwilling to go: first they took the young and strong men, making them march at the head of the first convoy; the women, old men, and children followed; some of the most determined fled into the depths of the forests near the river Saint-Jean, a region heretofore unexplored. The executers of this barbarous order were unmoved by their prayers and tears, and eighteen thousand Frenchmen were thus torn from their fertile and well-cultivated lands, despoiled of all they possessed, separated from their families,—for they divided them into bands without taking into account the ties which bound them together,—and carried into the most remote provinces. Humiliated, poor, and in despair, they were thrown in the midst of Protestants, enemies of their religion, their country, and their manners, customs, etc., without knowing the fate of those from whom they were separated or the least hope of ever seeing them.

There is a very curious fact attached to this lamentable history: some of these unhappy people, as I told you before, escaped on the shores of the river Saint-Jean, and no more was heard of them until fifty years after, when England and the United States were disputing their boundaries in Canada, it became necessary to explore those parts of the country mentioned in the Treaty of 1783, by which England acknowledged the independence of the United States. In 1803 some English and American engineers went to the river Saint-Jean to seek traces of the boundaries fixed by the treaty; and this doubtful boundary is a matter of dispute to this day, and may cause a war between these two countries. You may imagine the astonishment of these engineers to find in a country always thought to be uninhabited a population of ten or twelve hundred Frenchmen, whose existence was unknown to the whole world. They had retained their customs and religion, and during a half century the Catholic clergy had sent them priests, and had kept the secret of their retreat so well that no one in England or the United States suspected their existence. After their discovery some retired into the forests, where they are still; others went to the United States or into the English possessions.

I saw Mr. Poinsett, the Minister of War, yesterday. He is a very sensible and intelligent man, and I shall regret him more than any one in the Administration, which seems to be cidedly lost; everything seems to announce the defeat of Mr. Van Buren and the success of General Harrison. This change will make no difference in the foreign politics of the country, but will probably have a very bad influence on the financial situation; neither party seems to worry about it, and only care to win the election without thinking of what it may cost: this is how they understand the love of one's country.

LIII.

WASHINGTON, September 19, 1840.

NOTWITHSTANDING the sadness that prevails here, the nights are so noisy that one can scarcely sleep: there is a continual uproar, the reason for which is that the inhabitants all own cows and pigs but no stables, and these animals wander about all day and night through the city, and go to their owners' houses only in the morning and evening to be fed; the women milk their cows on the sidewalk and sprinkle the passers-by. The nocturnal wanderings of these beasts create an infernal racket, in which they are joined by dogs and cats. An American to whom I expressed my astonishment at this state of things, and particularly at the freedom allowed the pigs in all the towns of the United States, said that nothing was more convenient or conducive to health; that without the aid of these animals the towns would be encumbered with filth of all kinds.

I went with M. de la Fosse to see the Falls of the Potomac: we travelled for four hours over the rockiest roads. These dark imbedded rocks produced a wonderful effect, but the Falls were very poor—mere threads of limpid water running down these imposing black masses of rock. The path which leads to the Falls is dangerous: one is obliged to pass from one rock to another on boards that are not safe, and through bushes filled with snakes.

I was just going to bed last night when Colonel Achille Murat, the son of the former King of Naples, was announced; he married an American and lives in Florida. He was in Paris last year and saw the King; he wishes to return to France to look after some claims he has there, and begged me to announce his coming to my Government. His bearing is certainly not royal: he is small and fat, with a protruding stomach, and wears gold spectacles, with more the appearance of a notary than of a Prince. However, they say he is very energetic: he is a colonel of militia, has been a lawyer, a judge, and a notary, and has had during his varied life numerous duels. He says that the State of Florida has been ravaged for four or five years past by a band of fifteen hundred Indians, who have kept the whole army of the United States in check.

This tribe, called Seminoles, and renowned for their ferocity, commit all kinds of atrocities: no one ever knows where they are; they fall unexpectedly on the homes of the planters, and massacre every one there without mercy. The inhabitants barricade themselves every night, and M. Murat makes his negroes mount guard by turns. He has left his wife alone there, and will be absent more than a year; he says jokingly that until now she has been his lieutenant, but has been promoted to the captaincy. The most of the planters have imported bloodhounds of an immense size from the Havanas. These dogs are noted for their acute scent and love of blood; they eat the Indians! Charming country to live in!

Two days ago I went for the first time to a ball, in Washington, at the house of Mrs. Meade, a Catholic, and very highly thought of here. I care very little for American parties. The mistress of the house is polite, but very common; she has three daughters, one of whom was married fifteen days ago. These women are badly brought up, badly dressed, and their hair badly arranged; they are *third-rate* English. I will make one exception and only one—in favor of the daughter-in-law of Mr. Van Buren, whose acquaintance I made at this ball: in any country she would be considered an agreeable woman, graceful and distinguished in manners. The Diplomatic Corps were there, and the best society of Washington. The reception-rooms were composed of two parlors made into one by large sliding-doors, much in use here, and a long and narrow gallery resembling a corridor, lined with frightful paintings, and at the end of this gallery the music, such as you would expect to find at a low tavern, perched on a platform; there was scarcely any light, and the whole appearance was pitiable. For refreshments, ices and Madeira wine—nothing more: so much the worse for those who were hungry; I beg to say distinctly that I was not. And this is the most fashionable house in Washington.

The affair of Lafarge and Léotaud is much talked of here. You have no idea how much harm we do ourselves abroad by the publicity we give to these affairs, and particularly in a democratic country like this: they rush after the French papers, and rejoice in probing this wound in the heart of our society. These people who would like to destroy all social distinctions which cannot profit them, desire to attach themselves to the English nobility, but will not admit the nobility of other nations; and their great interest in the Lafarge affair is not the assassination of the bourgeois husband by the bourgeoise wife, but the history of the diamonds which soil the names of Nicolaï and Leotaud.

The Morel affair is still remembered and talked over with malicious pleasure, and they draw the conclusion from these low crimes —thank God very rare—that our morals are frightful and our young girls badly brought up! This is painful to hear when far from home.

LIV.

The King having charged me to remember him to General Masson, and to assure him of his feelings of friendship toward him, I went three days ago with M. de Montholon to see him at his country place, twelve miles from here. This old gentleman was the King's guide in this part of the United States forty odd years ago. His wife received us, and he came in soon after, followed by his six daughters, dressed in black. They were all very agreeable, and what was astonishing, prodigious, enormous, they pressed us to stay to dinner—a politeness unknown to Americans, who never admit any one to their table without having made their preparations long time before, and drilled their negroes and negresses. An impromptu invitation was a great proof of their good-will. I refused, but promised to come some other time. The good General, who is sixty-five years old, begged me to thank the King for his gracious remembrance; he was transported with joy and gratitude.

I passed an evening tête-à-tête with poor

Mr. Van Buren, who considers his election lost, and attributes it to corruption and election frauds. He is right, but forgets that his party did the same thing on another occasion.

I went to see Mr. Paulding, the Secretary of the Navy, to thank him for information he had given me. I found him surrounded by a very common set of people. The conversation turned upon the attraction of American young *misses*. According to these good people, every stranger must fall in love with them. A poor devil of a bachelor like myself can go nowhere without hearing this tempting refrain.

M. Miollet showed me a very pretty map of the sources of the Mississippi, which he had worked at for several years. He informed me that Carolina had been named by Frenchmen, who had established the first colony there under Admiral Coligny, who called it Carolina, after Charles II. As to Virginia, it has for etymology the virginity of Queen Elizabeth of England!!!

I went last night to see Mr. Poinsett, Secretary of War. He has travelled a great deal, and has not the prejudices of his compatriots, who believe in the absolute perfection of the

American Constitution, notwithstanding which its reputation receives some rude attacks from all sides. M. de Tocqueville's book is in great danger of being thought nothing but a fabulous romance. The newspapers are filled with accounts of the most scandalous electoral frauds; the two parties who are contending accuse each other, and both with undeniable proofs. The moral corruption is equal to the political corruption. It is curious to see the gradual destruction of all these beautiful institutions, which they wish to impose on us in Europe, at the very moment that they are declining here after sixty years' trial.

LV.

WASHINGTON, November 2, 1840.

WE are now in the exciting week preceding the election, and will know in eight days who will be President of the United States. You cannot imagine what a fever every one is in: it is political excitement, boiling over with rage! The day before yesterday in Philadelphia the Van Buren party demolished the house which was the headquarters of the opposite party. There is no organized civil force in the United States, so the populace can go to any imaginable excess without fear of repression; time will probably make them feel the need of an armed force, and the day when this armed force shall have the preponderance in the country will be the end of the present Constitution. So I think if they are right in saying that kings will eventually be done away with, they will be able to say the same thing of republics in America. I console myself better with the one than the other.

LVI.

WASHINGTON, November 10, 1840.

MY friend Van Buren is beaten and General Harrison is victorious. The election will not, however, be decided for fifteen days yet, and the new President will not enter upon his duties until March 4, 1841. I am sorry on my own account at the result, which, besides, will be prejudicial to the country. The Democratic Party, which is in power now, has been directed by Mr. Van Buren and his friends with moderation and wisdom, but when it becomes the Opposition party it will put no bounds to its violence. The Whig Party (which is called that of the aristocracy—my God, what aristocracy!) will split as soon as they come into power, and the governmental machine will find itself opposed by a furious democracy. To give you an idea of the American Constitution, this is what is to take place after the new election. From this time to the 4th of March next Mr. Van Buren will hold the office of President, which puts him in a very ridiculous position in face of those who have taken the power away from him. Congress, in which he has a majority, will meet in December. Of course nothing will be done to aid the coming Administration, who in coming into power on March 4 will find, in the first place, the Treasury empty, and be able to do nothing until the following December, for Congress is irrevocably dissolved on the 4th of March, and they cannot call a new one until December, because new members must be elected during the interval. It seems to me that the old maxim, "The King is dead: long live the King," is better than these intervals, which open the door so wide to all sorts of disorder. Such a Constitution is vicious in its consequences as in its principle, in spite of the theories, more or less specious, of M. de Tocqueville.

Mr. Van Buren bears his defeat with dignity, and as they say here, with *fortitude*. General Harrison was born in the State of Virginia, which is thought the model State as regards pure republican principles, joined with good education and good manners. It is, in one word, the birthplace of *gentlemen*. Take notice, I beg of you, that I am only the reporter of public opinion, and that I do not guarantee the quality of these so-called *gentlemen*. Mr. Harrison left Virginia very early, as all these poor devils in that State do, to seek his fortune in the West. He settled in Ohio, and later entered the army, and was distinguished enough to be made a General, which does not signify much in America. He served without success from 1812 to 1814 against the English; afterward against the Indians, and his great exploit was a victory he gained over them at a place called Tippecanoe. He lost one hundred and fifty men, and killed three hundred of the enemy. And for that this conqueror has received the brilliant title of "The Hero of Tippecanoe;" and it is the refrain of all the songs, of all the pieces of prose and of poetry, in his honor, which have been plentiful during this past year. General Jackson, the predecessor of Mr. Van Buren, sent General Harrison back to his home, where, a new Cincinnatus, he has conducted his plough; he has also been notary in his village. The party opposed to Mr. Van Buren not daring to bring forward their most distinguished men, who are more brilliant than the Democrats, brought General Harrison from his obscurity to make him a candidate for the Presidency, and from that time he has become a great personage, and his sayings and doings are looked upon as important — *Americanly* speaking. Thus he said that he preferred his *log-cabin* — a house built with trunks of trees — to the palace of a king; and his log-cabin has become an emblem of the party: it is painted on all their flags; it serves as their banner everywhere; they have built one in the middle of

Washington. And there, for the last six months, the partisans of the new President have met and yelled speeches and songs. He also said that he drank nothing but hard cider, and not the foreign wines of the aristocrats. Since then it is not the proper thing to get drunk on anything but *hard cider*, and they have vaunted this drink in prose and in verse. He also said that his log-cabin had no lock, and that all good Democrats could come in and be welcome at any time; then Harrisonian hospitality became proverbial! To tell you all the stupidities that have been inspired by these poor sayings I have cited, during the last year, would be impossible. I have seen nothing, heard nothing, read nothing, in which the log-cabin or hard cider did not appear. The newest style in dress is called Tippecanoe, and the American women in everything they wear seek to do honor to the illustrious conqueror. Thanks to all these truly ridiculous proceedings, this General, not heard of yesterday, is elected to-day; and solely on account of his mediocrity, which they judge inoffensive, he is to occupy the first position, and govern the country during the next four years.

Opinions are divided on the course he will follow. Some say that, like Sixtus V., he will throw away his crutches, and putting aside those who have brought him into power, will rule with an ability that will astonish the universe. But most persons say that he is a vain man, without mind or talent, who will be a puppet in the hands of flatterers, and those who wish to control him will ruin the country while quarrelling amongst themselves. However, they say he is an amiable man, rather vulgar, and having the mania of quoting the Greeks and Romans, whom he knows nothing about, but thinks it good taste to appear to know.

We are buried in snow: in the same degree of latitude as Lisbon, we have the temperature of Sweden in winter and of the tropics in summer.

LVII.

WASHINGTON, November 25, 1840.

I HAVE accepted an invitation to dine with Mr. Seaton, proprietor and editor of the *Daily National Intelligencer*, the Opposition journal in Washington, and one of the best newspapers in the United States: it will be the official organ of the Harrison Administration. Mr. Seaton is also Mayor of the city. His paper has always been less hostile to France than the others. Six years ago, when we had some difficulty with the United States, he on several occasions opened its columns to our Legation. I did not wish to hurt his feelings by refusing his invitation, and thus deprive my mission of a useful auxiliary; besides, in this country almost all the more distinguished *gentlemen* are journalists.

Yesterday morning I went to see the Secretaries of War and Navy: they were feeling very sore about their defeat; they say the world has become ungovernable, particularly in those countries which have adopted constitutional forms, and other things of the same kind, which prove that sensible men in both hemispheres recognize constitutional institutions as only a special phase of human folly.

LVIII.

WASHINGTON, December 8, 1840.

EIGHT days ago I gave a grand dinner to Mr. Forsyth, the Secretary of State, who sent a regret just as we were sitting down to dinner after waiting more than a quarter of an hour. It appears that Americans think no more of this than of any other breach of politeness; and I have been assured that they never refuse until the last moment.

Our Consul at Lima has had a serious difficulty with the Peruvian Government. He challenged the Minister of Foreign Affairs to a duel, and he, knowing that M. Saillard, our Consul, had already killed two men, would not accept unless, according to Spanish custom, they fought on horseback and with lances. The President of the Republic interfered, and put the Minister under arrest, and placed a sentinel at the Consul's door, who protested, and threatened a blockade. This was the state of affairs when last heard from. We create difficulties for ourselves everywhere.

I have heard two things that have happened, that I give you as specimens of American manners. One occurred at the University of Richmond, capital of the State of Virginia. A revolt took place there six years ago, and the students celebrate the anniversary every year on the 12th of November by every sort of excess. Lately on this anniversary they disguised themselves, and went to the houses of the professors, among others to Mr. *Dairs*, one of the most distinguished men in the college. The moment he appeared at the door, a student drew a pistol and shot him dead. Notwithstanding the horror created by this crime, it is very probable that this young criminal will not be condemned.*

The other affair was equally bloody: A man in easy circumstances killed a workman with whom he had a discussion. He was put in prison, but offered a sum of six thousand dollars to be set at liberty provisionally, and immediately left the country. He went to

---

* Prof. Davis was shot at Charlottesville, not Richmond.

the West and bought land. He will become a rich man, and perhaps in a few years a member of Congress from the State in which he has settled. This has happened before. These facts are evidently the result of the infancy of the country, and prove that civilized countries had better not copy this.

I went yesterday to the Capitol to see the opening of Congress, which did not take place: the bad weather had prevented the members from reaching here. The roads are buried in snow, and it is even very difficult to walk along the streets. A train was stopped for twenty-four hours, not being able to go backward or forward, the passengers exposed to a bitter cold, with nothing to eat. One of them, a member of Congress, slipped from the platform and fell between the rails; the train passed over him without injuring him in the least. He had fallen at full length under the train and with his head in a hole, which saved him.

For some time past the mania for suicide seems to have become an epidemic in the Northern States, both among strangers and natives. Two weeks ago we heard of two cases—one a Frenchman, and the other a creole of Saint-Domingo, settled in this country, and in easy circumstances. Last week the papers of New York published among the suicides without any known cause that of a man sixty-three years old, Mr. Nathaniel Prince, one of the principal bankers of the city. The Philadelphia papers report the death of a young girl of eighteen, beautiful, modest, rich, and engaged to be married, who sawed through her throat with a razor full of notches, after having tried to poison herself twice with laudanum and arsenic. Public feeling is much excited; and the public press have sought to find some remedy for this social malady. An Albany paper and one in New York City have agreed that the old practice should be revived of dishonoring and anathematizing the bodies of suicides. They propose that the body should not be buried, but exposed, by the law, to abandonment and infamy. It is a violent remedy, whose philosophical legitimacy I shall not inquire into. In a country where liberty is the governing principle it seems as though it ought to understand and logically sanction the killing of one's self. I am certain that if this proposition should come before Congress to-morrow, logicians would be found there who would oppose it as an infringement on personal liberty guaranteed by the Constitution. Suicide would then become a subject of controversy. The moral malady is bad enough without aggravating it by political combinations; because the suicide is refused a tomb, it is not necessary to raise a monument for him.

But what are the causes of these suicides? Is there some common symptom in this disease by which so many people have been attacked, which can help to determine its character? I think there is. The victims of this unfortunate monomania all belong to the higher classes, and in easy circumstances; thus no other motive for their melancholy but a mysterious ennui. Ennui! that is to say the indifference, the egotism, which affects the American when he has everything to make him happy. He owes this terrible moral plague to his education, and to his domestic and social habits. American society is governed by self-interest. "Gain"—this is the aim of all their ambition. To attain it men associate their efforts and make their calculations together, without any interchange of sentiments, without any emotion. Their minds are isolated; nothing outlives the division of profits. After that all association is broken.

An American is never satisfied unless in constant action; as soon as he rests, whether because his fortune is made, or because he feels the weight of age, he becomes melancholy and unhappy. He remains alone and quiet in the midst of a society which is continually moving and where he counts for nothing; he succumbs to his uselessness, and particularly to the indifference and inattention of others. His life was in his business: in giving up one he gave up the other. Speculator, he had others interested in him; these were not his friends, but his companions; between them there was the commercial battle-field, which was also a kind of fraternity. The day he gives up his business this soldier of traffic is invalided. His inactivity finds no compensation in the enjoyment of his acquired riches; for in the United States the only enjoyment and the only occupation is the continual working of this money; once permanently invested, it loses all its value. These retired merchants die from neglect and loneliness, and from want of something to do in the midst of the stir and activity of every one around them. They don't find even in their own family the importance they have lost in the outside world. In America paternity is without prestige and old age without a crown. No one cares for him; the thoughts of his children are elsewhere, for they must in their turn work and speculate to increase their patrimony and enjoy it. There is a resemblance and a difference between the American and the miser: both materialize their earthly happiness by centring it on gold, but the happiness of one is in hoarding his dollars, the other in continually moving them. This materialization of all pleasure has made society in America cold, and has affected the marital relations even more. A married woman in the United States is only a machine to produce children, a wax figure covered with velvet; she has the right of maternity, and of spending her husband's money, but otherwise counts for nothing. She is treated with politeness, but made to feel her inferiority. Whether this stiffness in their social relations has its compensation in the sanctity of home I cannot say; but I fear that with the merchant love is completely stifled by preoccupations of business and politics. They take some notice of young girls, because they are something to get, to procure; but the woman has no place in American society. The prospect of marriage stripped of its poetry and tenderness is enough to frighten any one; it is only in America that young girls kill themselves who have not been disappointed in love and where shop-girls have the spleen. Nowhere but in this country do rich and worthy old men wish to cut off the few remaining days of their life!

Instead of making life, which is already so dismal in America, more so by legal penalties, instead of dwelling on all that is gloomy in the past on one side, and on the puritan Bible on the other, let them introduce, if it is possible, something joyous into their life—a little poetry and passion!

It is only necessary to stroll either in the country or through the streets of New York or some other city in the United States on a

Sunday, and watch the deathly silence of the inhabitants walking with closed mouths and gloomy faces, to understand that these people ook upon a gay life as they would on a funeral.

LIX.

WASHINGTON, December 25, 1840.

TWO hours before the meeting of the House of Representatives, and fortunately when no one was in the Hall, the chandelier fell and was broken into a thousand pieces. It was of an enormous size, cost twenty-five thousand francs, and had just been put up. This shows the incompetency of the workmen in this country, who never do anything thoroughly or well.

I have been to see Mr. Bancroft, who has just come from Boston. He is a great friend of M. Guizot and corresponds with him; he is one of the *eminent litterary characters* of the United States, of which he is now writing a history. I invited him to dinner, where he will find persons who share his opinions, for he is a partisan of the present Administration, —Democrat, or *lacofoco*, as they say here,— and my other guests are all of this party.

I have been struck with the difference in the length of the days in Europe and America. Last summer they seemed to be shorter than in Europe; now they appear longer. This is explained by the difference of ten degrees of latitude; but one feels it very much.

I made two new acquaintances at the Austrian Minister's yesterday. One of them, Mr. Calhoun, who is one of the most celebrated persons in the United States, has been the leader of a party called *multifiers*, who threatened eight years ago to separate the States of the South from those of the North, and thus destroy the Union. Mr. Calhoun is one of very few who are favorable to us, and oppose putting a high tax on our silks. He is from South Carolina, where the feeling toward France is better than in the other States.

My other new acquaintance was Mr. Sumter, representing also South Carolina. I sat next to him, and to my great surprise he thanked me for my kindness to his maternal grandmother, and I was not less astonished to hear that he was the grandson of the old Marquise de Lage, and brother of Madame de Fontenay. He is very well for an American, and I hope will defend our commercial interests.

Mr. Van Buren has sent his message to Congress. It is well written, and he had the good taste to make no allusion to his defeat. The song of the swan is in his case a song of triumph, so ably has he withdrawn himself from this miserable affair.

I went to a Charity Fair held by the "elegant ladies" of the city; it was only curious on account of the filth, the poor display and bad order kept. One half of the stands were filled with eatables, and these ladies served goose, ham, tea, coffee, and ices. Suitable to the American, who spends all the time he is not engaged in business in drinking and eating.

Here is a new story that will make you familiar with the tone of the society in which I have the pleasure and honor to live. A Mr. de Muhlenberg, of German parentage but born and brought up here, and in high position, since he has been United States Minister at Vienna for three years, was asked by one of his friends, in my presence, what he thought of Prince Metternich. He reflected, and would not answer at first. His friend insisted, and then he said, "You want to know what I think of Prince Metternich? Well, he is a hog!"

LX.

SOME days ago I went to an evening party at Mr. Gadsby's, proprietor of the hotel where I stayed on my arrival here, which he has relinquished to his son. He is an old wretch who has made a fortune in the slave-trade, which does not prevent Washington society from rushing to his house, and I should make my Government very unpopular if I refused to associate with this kind of people. This gentleman's house is the most beautiful in the city, very well furnished, and perfect in the distribution of the rooms; but what society, my God! It made my hair stand on end to find myself amongst these men and women rivalling each other in bad manners. I have never thought of the great importance of politeness in social relations, but now I see that it is the fundamental basis and the most indispensable element. The women, ridiculously dressed, stood around the room hanging on their husbands' arms. Perhaps it was very moral, but I assure you it was very grotesque. There are no young people in the French province who have not better manners. To change this state of things, these strange people will have to go abroad and see something of the best society in London and Paris; but this, I am afraid, would be difficult. Then they would copy us; for though extremely vain, they have all the instincts of the monkey in their desire to imitate, and allow themselves to be influenced by the masses, but look upon us isolated Europeans as lunatics because our manners and behavior are different from theirs.

You ask me what city in the United States I should dislike the least to live in? Without doubt, Philadelphia. Boston is too cold; New York too noisy, and full of adventurers from all parts of the world, who have to seek a fortune or an asylum; Baltimore is as gloomy as a tomb; while Philadelphia has an air of dignity, cleanliness, and gentility which makes it a place apart. One finds material resources of all kinds there, and a society which is agreeable. As to Washington, it is neither city, village, nor country: it is a great workshop, with building-materials everywhere, in a desolate situation, and where life is intolerable.

I went yesterday evening to a party at the house of the Minister of Russia, and was presented to Mrs. Webster, wife of an important person, or at least of a person who is much talked of. He is the most celebrated lawyer in Boston, and the greatest orator in the Senate, the busiest politician, and, it is said, intimate with, and advocate when well paid, of all bankers and financiers who have been brought before a court of justice for any crimes or misdemeanors. He is a great partisan of England, and consequently anti-French, and is spoken of as Secretary of State under the future President. He is said to be rough in his manners, wilful, and ill-bred. This promises pleasant diplomatic relations for me. Bates gave me a letter to him, which I sent immediately on my arrival here, but as yet have not had an opportunity to make his acquaintance.

LXI.

WASHINGTON, January 12, 1841.

I HAD heard that the President's public receptions on New Year's Day were so very ridiculous that I anticipated some amusement; but there was nothing of the kind. I arrived at the appointed hour, eleven in the morning, with M. de Montholon and M. de La Fosse. After waiting a few minutes we were ushered into another room, where we found Mr. Van Buren with the members of his Cabinet and their wives and children. After the customary *shake hands* and some complimentary words to each, very happily expressed by Mr. Van Buren, we watched the arrival of a great many men, some of whom were very common-looking and very much embarrassed at finding themselves in such beautifully furnished rooms.

It is an established custom that on the first day of the year the sovereign people have the right to enter the President's House and make themselves perfectly at home. Some years ago even the hackmen who brought people to see the President went up after them, and whip in hand made the tour of the rooms. Nothing of this kind took place, or anything showing American peculiarity; it was only dull and second class. The Diplomatic Corps made a rather ridiculous figure, being the only persons in uniform; the crowd who were wandering around the rooms examined us as if we were curious wild beasts.

I went to a ball at Mr. Forsyth's, Secretary of State. This entertainment was pretty good, compared to those I have been to before. They waltz seldom, and when they do, very badly. The quadrilles are danced without either grace or animation. I saw the acknowledged beauty of Washington, Miss Mason, tall, light blonde, and regular features, but dressed like a doll such as you see at the fairs in the provinces sold at thirty-five cents.

I went to the President's yesterday to give him a letter from the King announcing the birth of the Duc de Chartres; we talked for a long time about European affairs, of which he did not understand one word. If I did not know how ignorant Europeans were of the United States I should be surprised at the ignorance of the people here about our old world. We returned to American affairs; on this subject Mr. Van Buren is remarkable, and the more earnest because he feels bitterly his defeat.

The state of affairs in this country now is such as to draw the attention of Europe to it; for a long time there have been questions in suspense between the United States and England about their respective boundaries; many collisions have taken place between the English and American *borderers*, and a fresh one is dreaded which may bring on war between the two countries. Although this is the general opinion, I do not think it is as bad as that. Lord Palmerston and his representative, Mr. Fox, treat the Americans with hauteur and insolence such as Europe has had experience of. The new Administration which goes into power the 4th of March is altogether English at heart; and will without doubt immediately make concessions which will insure the maintenance of peace.

I have just received an invitation to a *wedding-ball* at General Macomb's; under the seal there is a knot of white satin—singular custom!

I was obliged to visit Congress yesterday to

talk over with several members business matters in which my Legation was interested, for here diplomatic affairs are not treated as everywhere else, where we communicate with the Minister of Foreign Affairs and arrange the matter with him alone. On the contrary, here the Minister submits the questions to the President, who decides whether to admit them. When he decides in the affirmative, he sends them to the Senate and to the House of Representatives, whence they are sent to the different committees whose business it is to examine and report on them. The *chairman* or president of the committee then reports to the House, who then vote for or against it. The result of this is that the diplomatic agent is obliged first to see the Secretary of State and explain the affair to him, then the chairman to interest him in the question and to persuade him to consider it favorably, and then to see each of the most important members of Congress and try to convince them. The delays are interminable. There are three affairs which have been hanging on for three years, and I am anxious to have them settled during the present session.

I have seen Mr. Clay, the great man of the country, who will be still greater, as they say he will be the director of General Harrison, and candidate of his party for the next Presidency. He was particularly polite to me, probably on account of the reputation his party have for being anti-French. I had only seen him once before—in the month of July. He repeated at the Russian Minister's what he had told me before, that he had been badly received by the elder branch of the Bourbons when he was in Paris in 1814. Is it not delightful to see a democrat who has been badly received by a king nurse this grievance for twenty-six years! He was, however, very anxious to show his high opinion of the present King, praising his great intelligence, his liberal ideas, and "finding him worthy of governing a republic."

LXII.

WASHINGTON, January 22, 1841.

I DINED yesterday with the Austrian Minister. The celebrated Mr. Webster was there; he is *pompous* to the last degree, and ill at ease. I still think that all the distinguished men in this country would be only second or even third class in England. They give themselves the airs of importance one sees in the brewers of London, with their vanity, vulgarity, and absurdity. As to Mr. Clay, he is of another type—that of a *gentleman farmer*.

I went to a *wedding-party* at General Macomb's; a crowd compressed into two small rooms; common people, and detestable music. I will not speak of the melted ices, which flowed everywhere, and of the hot wine, the odor of which was very strong. I did not taste it.

I met at Colonel Totten's, the Director-General of the military works, and former colleague and friend of General Bernard, a very curious couple — *General and Mrs. General Gaims*, as they call them here. The husband is one of the numerous candidates for the next

Presidency. For the last three months he has been going from city to city giving lectures or speeches on the art of war and means of defence in the United States. This is not at all uncommon in this country; but to see his wife succeed him on the same platform and give lectures on the blessings of peace, is as curious here as elsewhere. *Mrs. General Gaims* is a little woman, whose head scarcely reaches to her husband's shoulder, to whom she clung all the evening. She is frightfully ugly, with a red face covered with blotches; and, to add to this, she had arranged her hair in little rings plastered all over her head and brow. She is a real monster. One could laugh at this curious object, if he could retain spirit enough in this dreary country to laugh at anything.

I gave a dinner yesterday. Amongst my guests was Mr. Calhoun, who is opposed to the present Administration. He has better manners than his colleagues in the Senate, and has the merit of being a declared enemy of a high tariff on our silks and wines. Mr. *Hunster* was also one of my guests. He has great influence in Virginia, where just now there is a great cry against France on account of the monopoly of tobacco which they say will diminish the consumption. I tried to prove to Mr. *Hunster* that this was not so, and although he seemed satisfied with my explanations, I found him *a very vulgar* person. Another of my guests was an influential member of Congress. This agreeable and distinguished man blew his nose in his napkin constantly during dinner! It is necessary to be civil to these savages, for they are the *leaders* on whom depend in a great measure the commercial interests I have to defend.

LXIII.

WASHINGTON, February 7, 1841.

I DINED lately with Mr. Van Buren. There were thirty guests, amongst whom, much to my astonishment, were Messrs. Clay and Webster, the two principal leaders of the Opposition, and most violent enemies of Mr. Van Buren, and who were certainly the most instrumental in his defeat. The disdainful Mr. Webster became more human, and approached me with some show of courtesy. I feel sure that by keeping a reserved manner toward him I should make him more civil: it is the same with the Americans as with the English—one must never make the first advances.

An earthquake was felt a few days ago at New York, and because it happened on the day of General Harrison's departure from his home—which is nine hundred miles from New York—to go to Washington, all the newspapers cried out, A miracle!

Mr. Clay made a speech in the Senate denying that he was hostile to France, of which he had been accused. He introduced a pompous eulogy of King Louis Philippe, "who had the honor of being the elect of the people and not one of those idiot kings, reigning by the absurd right of legitimacy." Unfortunately Mr. Clay, notwithstanding this strong eulogy, spoke against admitting our wines and silks without an augmentation of duty, and I strongly fear that he will succeed, as in a few months his party will be in power and have the majority in Congress.

I also heard a brawler speaking against our system of taxation: there is every reason to believe that I shall be beaten, but I shall not fall without defenders; I have furnished our friends with good arms, and they have recruited help from the opposite ranks, amongst others Mr. Wise, an orator of talent, who spoke the other day for four hours in our favor.

I went to see Mr. and Mrs. Charles Hill, who live at the extreme end of the city; my carriage sunk up to the axle-tree in the snow and mud; it was necessary to leave the carriage, which had to be dragged out and scraped to remove the mud and slush which stuck to it like glue. I don't know how any one can get to the Hills' on Monday next, when they give a ball; they count on the moon shining on that night to save their necks. This is how it is in Washington—streets not paved, swept, or lighted.

I went to a ball at Mrs. Woodbury's; the chandelier with three lamps not giving sufficient light, a hoop with candles on it had been attached. This piece of machinery broke down and fell amongst the dancers, happily without setting fire to the dresses of the *misses*.

Here is a Parliamentary incident which is

worth recording. Mr. Duncan, a member of Congress from Ohio, having presumed to question the courage and glory of General Harrison, Mr. Johnson from Maryland asked if the individual could not be called to order, who after having been branded as a coward in this House, dared accuse General Harrison of cowardice. Mr. Duncan did not hear this insult, but next day, seeing an account of it in the newspaper, he rose up and cried out, "I declare that I never heard these words attributed to Mr. Johnson, and I ask of the President if they were heard by him?" The President replying in the negative, Mr. Duncan continued: "Then, if these words have been uttered here, they were spoken low purposely that they might not be heard by any one, and he who has not dared to say them to my face is not only a vile liar, but a base blackguard and infamous coward!" Mr. Johnson pretended not to hear this violent attack on account of the great noise at the time; but seeing it in the newspapers next day, Mr. Johnson protested against the record of it, in the sitting of the day before, and demanded that it should be expunged, as the insults as recorded had never been given by Mr. Duncan. The latter not being present the request of Mr. Johnson was granted, and the House passed to the order of the day. Mr. Duncan carried the quarrel into the papers, where these gentlemen exchanged insults worse, if possible, than those in the House. This is what the beautiful forms of democracy lead to.

We all met at the Russian Minister's to consult as to what we should do on the arrival of General Harrison, who is expected every day. I advised that we should only leave our cards on him, as in my opinion anything more would be, if not an insult, certainly a want of delicacy to Mr. Van Buren. I was very much astonished to find that every one agreed with me, for my colleagues are all Harrisonians. So it was arranged as I had proposed.

LXIV.

WASHINGTON, February 21, 1841.

I WENT to a grand ball, called here *the Assembly*, where I remained about twenty minutes. They have one every fortnight; there are four during the winter. My colleagues and I all subscribed; these four pleasures only cost us one hundred francs each. Always the same society, or rather the same assemblage, but this time in a hall entirely too large and where one is frozen; and the wind blowing through it with such force that it caused the lamps to smoke.

There has been also a grand ball given by subscription to General Harrison, to which the Diplomatic Corps were invited. As it was an affair of party, I said to those of my colleagues who asked my advice, that I should not go; that there could be for us but one President until March 4—Mr. Van Buren. I believe that the Ministers of Russia and Belgium were the only ones who went.

I go every now and then to Congress to note the uselessness of their idle talk; it is pitiable! Just now they are on the chapter of economy, and no government costs more than this: each State has the expense of an entire government, independent of which the Federal Government costs them a great deal of money; each member of Congress, Senator, or Representative costs them, first, eight dollars for every twenty miles they travel to come from their home to Washington, and most of them have fifteen to eighteen hundred miles to go; they pay them the same to return; and they receive eight dollars a day for eight or nine months: there are three hundred and fifty of them. Add to this the costs of keeping the buildings in order, light and heat, expenses of all kinds, which are enormous, the total for the expense of the Senate and House of Representatives is more than five millions! I assure you their work is not worth it.

To kill the time, which passes slower at Washington than anywhere else, I write long dispatches, which unfortunately have not the interest or variety of the European correspondence, for in Europe the interests of all the great powers are complicated: they consult amongst themselves before taking any important step, and European politics are, so to say, a grand mechanism, where every part has its use and function. America offers nothing like it: all the States are too much occupied by their own affairs to interfere with those of other governments, and the United States have made themselves independent of European politics. When it is a question of recognizing a new sovereign in a foreign country, they have established a new order of things— they consult their own interests, and never follow the example of others; thus they were the only ones to acknowledge Don Miguel King of Portugal. They love or feign to love those governments favorable to their own principles, but do not quarrel with those whose system is different, and without approving of their political theories, they draw every advantage possible from their relations with them, and recognize those powers they think firmly established.

But if the spirit of isolation which the United States have sought up to this time to maintain in all questions of balance of power, or the manner of government and systems of alliance of European nations leave a poorer field for diplomatic correspondence, and prevents it from discussing questions to which this country remains indifferent, the interior situation of the United States is of itself remarkable enough to furnish various subjects of observation. It is indeed wonderful to see a State which has not been in existence more than half a century, and which has quintupled her population, extended her boundaries from the Atlantic to the Pacific, and from the great lakes of Canada to the Gulf of Mexico, which has multiplied its navigation and its means of interior communication, has created a respectable navy, carried its commerce to every part of the world, etc., etc. . . . Only considering the United States from this point of view, one has curious subjects of study; but I do not feel that I have the capacity to fill the rôle of a far-seeing and prophetic observer.

LXV.

WASHINGTON, March 10, 1841.

FANNY ELSSLER has made such a great impression at Havana, that on the day of her benefit the ladies gave her a purse containing fifty thousand dollars. They gave her a ball, to which she went in a chariot covered with flowers. The whole town went mad, crying "*la divina Fanny!*"

I have been to see Mr. Van Buren at Mr. Gilpin's, the former Attorney-General, with whom he has been living since he left the Presidential palace. He will stay there until his departure for New York City, whence he will return to his home in the country.

There was a curious exhibition yesterday, which gave a very just idea of *American manners*. All the Diplomatic Corps were to be presented to the new President. We all assembled beforehand at Mr. Fox's, the English Minister, except our colleague, the Russian Minister, who pretended to be sick, in order to obtain a private audience. From there we went to the Presidential palace. We had agreed upon the speech which Mr. Fox was to make in our names. On our arrival at *White House*, as they call the President's house, the new Secretary of State, Mr. Webster, who was very awkward in his functions, made his arrangements with Mr. Fox, after which we were placed in line against the wall, by rank, according to the time of residence here, and after a long time for a country where the chief of the Government has no right to keep any one waiting, the old General came in, followed by all the members of his Cabinet, who marched in single file and so stood behind him. He stepped toward Mr. Fox, whom Mr. Webster named to him. Mr. Fox read his address to him; then the President put on his spectacles and read, in his turn, his reply. Then, after having made *shake hands* with Mr. Fox, he walked from one end of our line to the other, giving each of us *shake hands* without saying a single word. This ceremony ended, he returned to the room he had come from and brought Mrs. Harrison, widow of his eldest son, whom he presented to the Diplomatic Corps in a body. Mr. Webster, who followed him, then presented Mrs. Finley, mother of this Mrs. Harrison, in the following words: "*Gentlemen, I introduce to you Mistress Finley, the lady who attends Mistress Harrison,*" and take note, this good lady who "*attends the others*"—takes care of the others—is blind. Then, suddenly, a crowd of people rushed into the room: they were the sisters, wives, daughters, cousins, and friends of the President and his ministers, whom they introduced to us, and *vice versa*, in the midst of the greatest confusion; most of the men who accompanied the women wore frock-coats.

It was evident that the poor Diplomatic Corps were destined to serve as food for the curiosity of these male and female boobies. Seeing this, after exchanging a few words with Mrs. Webster, the wife of the new chief, I hurried home.

There was another scene quite equal to this at the *State Department Foreign Office:* it was told me by M. Martini, chargé d'affaires of Holland. Thinking that it was the proper thing to make his first visit to the Secretary of State at his office, he went there a few days ago; he was shown into Mr. Webster's room, who was surrounded by a dozen political friends.

After saying, "*How do you do*," he showed him into the next room, the door of which was open, and said, "*There are the ladies.*" M. Martini found Mrs. Webster and ten other ladies, who told him they had come to examine the *State Department;* they then went out by another door, leaving him alone. He went back into Mr. Webster's room, who continued his conversation with his friends without taking the slightest notice of his presence, and M. Martini was obliged to leave without speaking of the official business which had been the object of his visit. This gives an idea of the people we have to deal with, and of the etiquette of the American Government.

LXVI.

WASHINGTON, March 28, 1841.

I SOMETIMES go to the Senate, where I hear and see things which are inconceivable. They are having sessions now which they call Executive, because the Senators confirm the nominations made by the President, who has just changed all the members of the Cabinet, and will change the most of the office-holders in the country, and all these nominations must be confirmed by a majority of the Senate. The first question which has occupied them is the change of Government Printer; this has caused a most violent discussion, which has lasted five days. One of the most respectable Senators, Mr. King of Alabama, who is one of the party opposed to the present Government, defended the character of the late Printer, which had been violently attacked by Mr. Clay, who, affecting to see in this a personal attack against himself, cried out that what Mr. King had said was false, cowardly, and infamous! Mr. King replied that he had nothing to say in answer to such words, but next day sent a challenge to Mr. Clay. The authorities of the city interfered, and put them under bonds to keep the peace within the District. This Parliamentary incident gives an idea of the tone of the Senate—the highest body in the United States, noted for its intelligence and for the consideration it enjoys. Mr. Clay is sixty-four years old and has been in public life thirty-four years, and looked upon as the most eminent man in the country. Mr. King is sixty years old. He is a Senator, and has filled many important offices.

There is in New York a Madame Restell, who sells powders to "ladies married or single," for the purpose of producing abortion. A lady who was dying, Mrs. Purdy, confessed to her husband that her malady was brought on by Madame Restell's treatment, not only in administering these powders, but by causing an operation to be performed upon her by an accomplice, after which she felt that she was dying. It was not till after this fact, and the death of the victim, that Madame Restell was arrested. Until now the jury had rejected all complaints, although for many years she had pursued this infamous practice, publishing in the newspapers the most curious and indecent advertisements, notifying 'ladies, married and single, "who feared to lose their reputation by giving birth to illegitimate children, or their beauty by having too many." Such things are more inconceivable in a country affecting great prudery. The New York papers say that there was found at Madame Restell's five or six hundred letters from "ladies, married and single," of the city and other places, asking advice, and thanking her for past services.

LXVII.

WASHINGTON, April 2, 1841.

OUR new President is sick, and is so much worse to-day that his life is in danger. No President has ever died whilst in power; the post of Vice-President has always been looked upon as insignificant, and the man who occupies this supposed sinecure was only nominated after the refusal of several others. Now he will find himself President for the next four years, as ordained by the Constitution; and this unlooked-for change causes great excitement in the country. It will have no influence on our relations, and will not prevent the extra session of Congress. The Vice-President is Mr. Tyler of Virginia, where the Administration of General Harrison has met with opposisition, but the general opinion is that Mr. Tyler's tendencies are more Harrisonian than Virginian.

LXVIII.

WASHINGTON, April 5, 1841.

GENERAL HARRISON died yesterday. He commenced his term on the 4th of March. His reign has lasted just one month, and the poor old man has had nothing but cares and worries during this month of responsibility. His death unsettles all that had been decided upon by the leaders of the victorious party and the conquered, Mr. Van Buren's party, will begin to agitate again. The funeral takes place on the day after to-morrow, and of course the Diplomatic Corps are invited.

LXIX.

Washington, April 12, 1841.

The funeral took place on the 7th. The procession started from the President's house, and proceeded on a walk four miles to the cemetery. The ceremonies and the funeral oration passed off in the most proper manner, which is to be noticed in this country, where everything else is very strange. The obsequies lasted altogether about five hours.

Mr. John Tyler is a widower, but has a son who is married, and his wife will do the honors of the Presidency. This young woman was formerly an actress, and has played in the theatre in Washington under the name of Miss Cooper; I had the imprudence to say that she would represent* very well. The next day it was repeated to her. What a singular country, where a woman can pass from the boards of a theatre to a kind of scaffolding which serves as a republican throne!

I paid a visit to Mr. Southard, Vice-President of the Senate, who, according to the Con-

---

* In French means both represent and act.

stitution of the United States, will replace Mr. Tyler in case of his death; he is a man of middle age, whose manners are better than those of the present generation.

LXX.

WASHINGTON, April 25, 1841.

ALL the Diplomatic Corps went to present their respects to the President for the first time. In the absence of Mr. Fox, who was sick, Mr. Bodisco made the address. Mr. Tyler made a very appropriate reply, then came forward, and gave a *shake hand* to each of us, accompanied with a short speech. What he said to me I will repeat in as near his own words as possible: "I am delighted to make the acquaintance of the French Minister, who comes from a country to which we owe much, and to which we are united by the bonds of gratitude. I shall endeavor to establish intimate and friendly relations with you, sir, who have had the advantage of living in intimate relations with the most distinguished diplomat in the whole world and of all time.

King Louis Philippe and Prince Talleyrand while living here obtained the right of citizenship, and America is proud to count them amongst her citizens."

I give you the exact words of the President, and I hope that you will be satisfied. As to me, I am always happy to find myself under the protection of a name and a souvenir that I cherish and respect. Mr. Tyler conducted himself during this audience in a manner to satisfy every one; without being a man of genius, he is thought to be greatly superior to General Harrison.

LXXI.

WASHINGTON, May 7, 1841.

I WENT to a very curious entertainment, which they called a *May Ball*. It is given by Mr. Carusi, the dancing-master of all the young girls in town. He keeps a public school, and in the month of May of each year these young ladies always elect one of their number " Queen." She is not chosen for her beauty, nor for her talent in dancing, but for her amiability to her companions, and her popularity among all these little girls from six to sixteen years old. The one put upon the throne the other evening was very ugly. She is the daughter of a doctor, who appeared enchanted. The ball commenced at eight o'clock; shortly after the queen made her triumphal entry. Cords had been stretched the length of the hall to protect the line of march. At a given signal the music played a National march, the doors were opened, and the procession filed in: first the smallest marching in step two by two; then a little *boy* about two feet high carrying a velvet cushion, on which was the white crown for the queen; she followed, leaning very ungracefully on the arms of two companions, and behind her the whole troop arranged according to height. They conducted the queen in this way to the platform prepared for her at the end of the room, she mounted the steps, and it was immediately filled by all the little people of this little court. Then a young girl as ugly as the queen herself approached her young Majesty and made a speech appropriate to the occasion, to which the queen answered; after which the orator placed the crown on the head of the sovereign, who was on her knees before her. The queen then got up and seated herself in the chair placed on the platform in imitation of a throne! A throne in America! The tableau was very satisfactory; these blonde heads with wreaths of roses gave an aspect of youth and gayety, so in contrast with American gloom.

I dined with General Macomb the day before yesterday, and sat next to Mrs. Tyler, the daughter-in-law of the President, and formerly an actress named Cooper; they praise her beauty and elegance in the highest terms, but without any reason. The American toilets are in very bad taste, and the fashion seems to be that of France twenty years ago. Mrs. Tyler has nothing either in her manners or speech which would remind any one of the stage; she embraced this career only to satisfy the wishes of her family and against her own feelings. She is simple and natural, without much intelligence. She has a child-like way of saying little things which are rather amusing; she knows no one yet in Washington. I made her talk about Williamsburg, a little town in Virginia where she has lived for the last three years. She complains that in this country married women are never invited anywhere, and that a *bachelor* never dares to speak to them, and says that out of Washington and New York the position of American married women is like that of the Pariahs. She has some of the prejudices of her country, amongst others that of thinking that Americans speak English better than the English themselves, and added "than the English of *high fashion* in London." Altogether, she is a little woman who appears to be a very good fellow.

I have just heard that Mgr. de Forbin-Janson, formerly Bishop of Nancy, and wandering preacher in the United States, is about to build a French church and French hospital. I sent this turbulent Bishop my modest personal offering of five hundred francs, and will write to Paris asking the aid of Government. Subscriptions from the King and Queen would make a good impression here, and I shall recommend it.

LXXII.

Washington, May 18, 1841.

President Tyler has just ordered a National fast of twenty-four hours on the occasion of General Harrison's death. Do you not think that it is a very singular idea, in a Protestant republic, to make a whole nation fast on account of the death of their Chief Magistrate? It seems to me a penance altogether arbitrary, and useless in a country where Protestantism does not admit the efficacy of prayers for the dead. This official fast is explained only by the passionate desire to make an effect and to show a religious feeling, which in fact served as a base to the first little republics of New England, but which has very much cooled down since that time.

Mr. and Mrs. Bates have arrived from London; after twelve years' absence they were anxious to see this country again. These are the first familiar faces I have seen since my arrival here. They imagine that everything has changed for the worse in America, but I think that their European habits have very naturally had a great influence on their impressions. Mrs. Bates finds the hotels dirty, the means of travelling insupportable, the people ill-bred, and her husband says that business men have all become *rogues, rascals*, and that the country is dearer than England. This is the judgment of two intelligent and reasonable Americans on their own country.

LXXIII.

WASHINGTON, June 6, 1841.

I TAKE a walk every morning at six o'clock to avoid the oppressive heat, and to-day at this unusual hour I met Miss Meade, one of the beauties of Washington, alone in the street, going or coming from I do not know where. Free manners!

We were invited by M. Martini to enjoy the moonlight on his terrace; the Diplomatic Corps went on foot. A terrific storm came on so suddenly, that hosts and guests were wet to the skin in an instant. We left in torrents of rain, with lanterns to light us on our way, and each one hurried to his home. But this storm has not cooled the air. One cannot find a shady place to walk in : the streets are so broad, the houses so low, and trees so scarce that everywhere one is broiled by the sun.

I have just come from Mr. Clay's, the great man of the country, who holds the majority of Congress in his hands, and it is by him that will be decided the financial questions brought before the Senate during this session. Again, he showed very kind feeling toward France and great admiration for the King, and was very amiable to me; but notwithstanding his fine words, I felt that there was behind all this the same determination : "We want money, and we cannot raise it except by taxation on foreign merchandise; everything which comes into the United States pays duty, except French silks and wines, which are luxuries; they must submit to the general law. To make these duties as moderate as possible is all that can be done." I see plainly that these duties are imposed from necessity, and not from any feeling of hostility, and I hope France will see it in the same light.

I was present at a scene lately which merits being told : I went to see the Secretary of the

Treasury, and was shown into an ante-room, where a ragged beggar asked me for alms. After a quarter of an hour in his company, I went into Mr. Ewing's room; he excused himself very politely for having kept me waiting, which is the more remarkable as he is a self-made man: at eighteen he could neither read nor write, and his nature must be a very superior one that, from such a starting-point, he should have reached the post he now occupies. He had only exchanged a few words when three of his colleagues—Mr. Crittenden, Attorney-General; Mr. Bell, Secretary of War; and Mr. Badger, Secretary of the Navy—came in: Mr. Badger smoking a cigar, which he did not extinguish; Mr. Bell laid down on a sofa, with his feet over the arms, and thus presenting the soles of his boots to us; as to Mr. Crittenden, finding it too warm he took off his coat, and pulled a great roll of tobacco from his pocket, put it in his mouth, and commenced chewing. They were very merry and facetious, and as I did not wish to hurt the feelings of men who were so influential in commercial questions, I joined in with them.

I visited the Patent Office this morning.

This establishment was originally intended for models of machines for which the Government had given patents, but they have ended by piling up a mixture of all sorts of things—costumes of the savages, birds, stuffed fish, pell-mell with treaties signed by the United States and Louis XVI., and countersigned by M. de Talleyrand; with uniforms, collections of buttons, skins of beasts, and insects! It is the most original Museum I ever saw.

They have voted to give twenty-five thousand dollars, which is one year's salary of the President, to the widow of General Harrison.

LXXIV.

Washington, June 21, 1841.

The Comte de Menou presented me to one of his friends, Miss Harper, niece of Mrs. Caton, mother of the Marchioness of Wellesley and of the Duchess of Leeds, grand-niece of Mgr. Coroll, first Archbishop of Baltimore, dead in the odor of sanctity; her family and the Harpers are the best in the country. Miss Emily Harper was brought up at the Sacré Cœur in Paris; she seems to be a very pious young girl, and to wish that every one should be edified by her piety. She lives in Baltimore during the winter with her mother, who is a widow, and in summer in a very pretty villa in the island of New-Port. She is now alone and living with a friend of her mother, Mrs. Graham, also a widow, and mother of a very handsome young man, who they say may probably marry Miss Harper. M. Menou was very anxious to introduce me to this house, where he appears to be very much at home. These people have distinguished manners, and speak French very well.

LXXV.

WASHINGTON, June 29, 1841.

GENERAL MACOMB is dead, and the Diplomatic Corps were invited to attend his funeral. They placed us at the end of the procession, although we were in uniform, which made the discourtesy more marked.

I went to the theatre for the first time since I have been in the United States, for I do not count as representations the ballets of Fanny Elssler. It was abominable: I ran away after the first two acts of Hamlet. Nothing could be more sadly grotesque than this bad acting, with forced effects and overpowering tirades.

LXXVI.

WASHINGTON, July 5, 1841.

YESTERDAY was the anniversary of the Declaration of Independence of the United States, but as it fell on Sunday they put off until to-day the celebration of the annual holiday, and I have been kept awake since five o'clock this morning by the incessant noise of cannons and fire-crackers. That is the American fashion of showing their satisfaction; to them noise personifies joy!

I went yesterday to the Senate, where the day before there had been some scandalous scenes; they were making apologies and excuses, and promises of moderation: all this is so ridiculous and disgusting.

I gave a dinner last Friday to M. Barbezat, a French merchant and Consular Agent at

Galveston, in the new republic of Texas. This republic of one hundred and fifty thousand inhabitants is a regular nest of bandits. The description M. Barbezat gave of their manners, customs, and acts of violence made me thank my stars for having brought me only here. The United States seems a paradise to any one coming from Texas, where one cannot leave the house without being armed to the teeth. The Government is composed of brigands clothed with power. This is not so astonishing when one thinks that Texas has been settled by men who have escaped from the hands of justice in the United States, where justice is slow and mild enough.

LXXVII.

WASHINGTON, July 17, 1841.

I WENT day before yesterday morning, at five o'clock, with M. de la Fosse, Doctor Bénit, and M. Hulman, the Austrian Secretary of Legation, to visit Harper's Ferry, about one hundred miles from here—a place I have long wished to see. Mr. Jefferson in a little work, which is very much thought of here, called "Notes on Virginia," says that the view of Harper's Ferry is worth a voyage across the Atlantic. It was not possible to be so near and not visit it. The situation is remarkably beautiful. At the foot of a mountain which rises from a hollow, two rivers, the Potomac and the Shenandoah, join, the one forming cascades before uniting with the other, which flows slowly around some charming islands. On the horizon on every side are high rocky mountains. Unfortunately this magnificent spectacle is spoiled day by day by the progress of civilization. General Washington established a factory of arms there in 1794—the oldest in the United States. In the last forty years a great many houses have been built, and now they are digging a canal and opening a railway which will connect Baltimore with the Ohio River, more than three hundred and fifty miles across the Alleghany Mountains. All these works change the aspect of this country, which I like to imagine as it was a century ago, inhabited by peaceful Indians. I see them in the midst of this wild country hunting and fishing for their living, but now all this beauty is marred by the disagreeable noises of the factories. There is on one of these mountains a projecting rock on which Mr. Jefferson wrote the description of the country. In remembrance of this it is called Jefferson's Rock. When he was elected President of the United States, a detachment of troops stationed at Harper's Ferry, hearing that he was about to disband them, tried in vain to destroy this rock.

The manufactory of arms is a very poor one. The guns made there are very expensive, as everything is in the United States, where manual labor is so dear. The hotel, where every one who comes to admire the scenery stays, is a miserable low place, but when they found out who we were, they tried their best to serve us well, for notwithstanding their pretended passion for equality, Americans are very anxious to please any one they think of importance—generally to get money out of them, but sometimes from vanity, being very proud of having anything to do with what they call "celebrities."

LXXVIII.

WASHINGTON, August 11, 1841.

THE heat is so overpowering, that one is obliged to walk out only during the evening and part of the night. This is the time chosen by open-air orators. I saw one the other night, a member of the Temperance Society, whom I had met in some of the best houses in Washington, preaching on a platform supported by two barrels. He gave vent to his eloquence by yelling like a madman. What singular manners!

There was a rumor of a ministerial crisis in Washington, which caused great excitement. Three members of the Cabinet sent in their resignations to the President, who managed with great skill to bring about a reconciliation.

The bill was passed yesterday against us. There is nothing to hope for; the Senate will follow the example of the House. I have been the subject of discussion in Congress. Mr. Adams raised a question of privilege in regard to a communication I had made to the Secretary of the Treasury, of a memorial on our commercial relations, which he had sent to a committee of the House. I knew very well that this was not the form required, and that my communication should have been made to the Secretary of State, who is Minister of Foreign Affairs; but he had from the beginning referred me to his colleague of the Treasury, and as I had a particular reason for preferring this channel, I made use of it. They cannot blame me with any justice. As to Messieurs the Secretaries of State and Treasury, let them get out of it the best way they can: it is their affair. The discussion is favorable to France in this much, that it proves they are taking an interest in French commerce, notwithstanding what is said in some of the newspapers, who accuse the French Government and its agents of carelessness and ignorance. All this disturbance shows how disagreeable it is to have any negotiations with Americans, whose institutions are so badly combined that one never knows through whom or how to make official communications. The President, to whom I went to complain of this imbroglio, apologized very politely for my name having been mixed up with affairs to which I was a perfect stranger, and he blamed Mr. Adams very strongly for having provoked the discussion.

Things are getting very complicated. They say the President has vetoed the bill to create a National Bank. If that is done, all the present parties will be dissolved, and another party formed on other grounds. A caricature has been circulated representing the President seated at a table, holding a pen in his hand, ready to sign a large paper before him, and above is written, "To sign, or not to sign—that is the question." A large steamboat was entirely destroyed by fire on Lake Erie. Out of two hundred passengers only thirty were saved.

LXXIX.

WASHINGTON, August 14, 1841.

I SEE by the papers that the frigate Belle-Poule, commanded by the Prince de Joinville, is expected at New York. I hope she will not arrive for a week yet, for just now, as the grand crisis approaches, I cannot leave Washington. In two days they expect the return of the Bank Bill with the President's veto, which will create an excitement throughout the country. Nothing so serious has happened for a long time in the United States, and I cannot abandon my post at such a time.

A man from the State of Ohio has written to the Mayor of Washington that this city is threatened by a terrible earthquake, which will be preceded by a very remarkable event. At the very time the Mayor was reading the letter a water-spout destroyed the greater part of the public market and injured several houses. This was thought to be the precursor indicated by the writer of the letter; and last night all the negro population and many of the whites went some distance from Washington to sleep. As to me, I remained quietly in bed, as you may suppose. However, I ran a real danger, though of a different nature from the one expected: we have all been more or less poisoned by verdigris.

LXXX.

WASHINGTON, August 17, 1841.

A GREAT many Representatives and others invaded the Senate Chamber yesterday. The President's Message announcing his veto of the Bank Bill was read in the midst of great excitement. There was much applause and one hiss; the man who hissed was drunk. Instead of arresting him, as they wanted to do at first, they contented themselves with putting him out of the hall. The sitting had nothing imposing about it: they seemed more inclined to joke about it than to be angry, and the crowd dispersed very quietly. That same evening I went to see the President, to inform him of my intention of going to New York to await the arrival of the Prince de Joinville. I found Mr. Tyler completely overcome by the feverish state of excitement in the country, and all that had taken place.

LXXXI.

Philadelphia, August 27, 1841.

I HAVE been so sick from our poisoning that I was not able to leave Washington until yesterday; luckily my young Prince is not in New York. I cannot take a step without meeting Fanny Elssler. I thought she had gone back to Europe, and I find her here, where she is going to dance.

LXXXII.

New York, August 29, 1841.

NO one knows anything about the arrival of the Belle-Poule; so I shall hasten my trip to Niagara before the season becomes too advanced, and profit by the company of Doctor Benit, that I may not be obliged to go alone. The time for his departure to South America approaches, unfortunately. I shall regret this excellent man very much.

LXXXIII.

ALBANY, September 1, 1841.

I LEFT New York at five o'clock this morning on a superb steamboat, which took me up the North River to this place in ten hours. This is one of the most beautiful rivers in the United States.

LXXXIV.

SYRACUSE, September 2, 1841.

WHAT do you say to this pompous name? Many others just as pretentious are to be met with in every part of the United States. Since seven o'clock this morning, when I left Albany, I have in travelling one hundred and sixty miles passed through cities and villages named *Schenestady*, Amsterdam, Francfort, *Palatine*, Rome, Manheim, *Onesda*, Manlius, *Uttica*, and all that to arrive at Syracuse, where I am very badly lodged. But I cannot tell you all the pleasure I felt yesterday in following the course of the Hudson; it is far more beautiful than the Rhine. It is true that this river of the New World has none of the historic souvenirs of the Rhine, which interests you with its ruins and legends. The history attached to the banks of the Hudson is of a kind entirely different. I passed by the place where Major André, the English spy, was hung; further, the spot where Arnold met the English officer. Albany is a very beautiful city, built in the form of an amphitheatre; there are several palaces—for the Legislature, for the courts of justice, and for the Government; for Albany is the capital of New York, and has forty thousand inhabitants. This morning we passed through the ravishing valley of the *Mohawek* River, which winds through this valley in the most picturesque manner; sometimes the route is so narrow, that the four different ways of communication touch each other, for there are following a parallel course the river, a superb canal, the railway, and a road. Sometimes the country is wild and absolutely uninhabited, then one perceives near the numerous falls on the river saw-mills and grist-mills. This valley of the *Mohawek* is the poetic ground in the history of the Indians: it is here that the tribe of the

Oneïdas lived, the *Ounwdagas* and the *Oswegas*; near here is Lake Cayuga, and not far off Lake Ontario, on which I embark this evening. But I am wrong in talking to you of the poetic remembrances of the Indians —to you who have so little enthusiasm for M. de Chateaubriand. There still remain a few unhappy descendants of this race: I met this morning at Oneïda five poor Indian women of the tribe of the Oneïdas; they offered to the passengers, in a suppliant manner, different objects worked in pearls. The Americans examined them, bargained, did not buy anything, and went away, saying, "Those things are perfectly useless; those people will never know how to make their living." Americans have no pity for the Indians, but accuse us of want of philanthropy in our war with the Algerians.

LXXXV.

CATARACT HOUSE, NIAGARA FALLS, September 5, 1841.

I HAVE at last arrived at this place, which is so renowned. I have seen, contemplated, and admired, but not with unmixed pleasure, as you will see by the following account. The day before yesterday I left Syracuse in a canal-boat, which is a kind of galiot like those which formerly went from Paris to St. Cloud; a means of transport which is the slowest, the most annoying and tiresome that one can imagine. There were forty-five of us, packed in the smallest space possible, elbowing and crowding each other, and suffering with the most intolerable heat, and this from nine o'clock in the morning to six in the evening. We went by the *Aswega* Canal, which runs between the shore of the lake of this name and the Senecca River. The country is very wild and rough, with woods and streams everywhere. Just as we arrived at Oswega the rain began to fall in torrents, with peals of thunder, and flashes of lightning to replace the light of the day, which had just ended. We were obliged to walk a mile through very deep mud, to reach the steamboat United States, which was waiting for us on Lake Ontario. We reached there covered with mud, and wet through. The lake was so rough that we were almost all sea-sick. It is seventy miles long, sixty broad, and two hundred feet deep; the storm produced a very beautiful effect.

I found M. Miollet and his travelling companion, M. Ducatel of Baltimore, on board. They had been detained three days at *Oswega* by a serious accident on the canal-boat. M. Ducatel had not lowered his head enough to pass under a bridge, and had his arm broken: lucky that he was not killed. This brave man is not very delicate, for he continues his journey with his arm bandaged, and will accompany M. Miollet down the Mississippi River. We shall probably separate this evening.

Our journey, which ought to have been over at six o'clock in the morning, was prolonged to noon—thanks to the storm. At last we araived at Lewistown on the Niagara River, where we took a carriage which brought us to Niagara Falls. The weather having become superb, we immediately descended one hundred and eighty steps to the banks of the river Niagara, from which place we could see the Falls from the American side, disappointing me so much that I already regretted having undertaken this fatiguing journey; but soon my admiration surpassed anything I could believe possible for any one to feel. We had crossed to the other side in a little boat,—the English side,—where we found a guide in a red dress. We were on British ground. We had climbed across rocks and frightful paths to a height parallel to that from which we had descended to the opposite shore. When we had reached the summit we were shown the celebrated places of the surrounding country: first, the battlefield where the Americans beat the English in 1813; then a spring of hydrogen, which ignited when brought in contact with a lighted candle; and last, the Table Rock, from which the Fall is seen.

It is the most magnificent spectacle, the grandest, the most solemn, the most gigantic, that I have seen in my life! After falling seventy feet, the river reaches a horseshoe of rocks, from which it falls one hundred and sixty feet, with immense waves and foam, and with a noise that nothing could give you an idea of. The water, green and brilliant as the emerald, flows rapidly toward the Fall, and loses itself in the snow-white foam, which is thrown up from the abyss in clouds of vapor, through which you could see nothing if it were not that a permanent rainbow, during the setting of the sun, pierces these white clouds and lightens every point. In one word, it is splendid and sublime! I cannot paint this magnificent scene, or describe the profound impression it made upon me. Humanity disappears entirely before a superhuman power. We were obliged to leave this unique spectacle sooner than we wished, as it was necessary to cross to the American side before the sun had set, or remain where we were until the next day. We stopped, however, a few minutes to see a live rattlesnake in a glass case, through which we could distinctly hear the noise he made whenever he moved his tail; it was like the sound of two rattles shaken together.

I also saw the barracks occupied by six hundred and fifty English soldiers who guard the frontier; the officers are most of them married, and live with their wives in little wooden houses scattered around the barracks. What a fate during six months of the year!—they have no other horizon than sky and snow.

We crossed again in our little boat, a quarter of a mile at most, from the Fall, and two hundred feet above the bottom of the abyss.

LXXXVI.

Buffalo on the Lake Erie, September 5, 1841.

AFTER writing this morning, I took Mr. Hooker, who has been a guide here for twenty-five years, and with Doctor Bénit and my valet, went to Goat's Island, which is on the American side and divides the Falls of Niagara. It is covered with magnificent trees, and there are beautiful views from different points. I went down two hundred steps to reach the lowest part of the Falls, and was then obliged to walk half a mile across stones and rocks, in the midst of clouds of mist. I jumped on to a rock underneath the fall, and sheltered in this way was able to see the torrents falling before me without any danger except of a bath, as the foam in evaporating made the atmosphere very wet. It was superb to find one's self below such a gigantic fall, *but a little frightful.*

We arrived at four in the afternoon at Buffalo, which is near Lake Erie. This city twenty-five years ago had only thirty houses; now the population is 40,000. Buffalo is called *The Queen of the Lakes.* The fact is that its present and future importance will not be one of the least wonders of the United States. Its situation is ravishing.

LXXXVII.

ROCHESTER, September 6, 1841.

I LEFT Buffalo this morning at seven o'clock in a stage-coach: nine of us were piled in, one on top of the other. We stopped at Batavia for dinner at three o'clock, and at five arrived here, after having travelled through one of the prettiest parts of New York State.

LXXXVIII.

Utica, September 7, 1841.

We travelled yesterday one hundred and fifty miles by railway through the lake country, partly along the shores of Lakes *Canaudaigna*, Seneca, Cayuga, *Owasco*, *Skuneatcles*, and Oneïda, one prettier than the other, and all bearing Indian names, while the towns are ridiculously called Geneva, Waterloo, Lodi, Victor, Palmyra, Byron, and Vienna. This country would be an ideal one if it was civilized according to our ideas, and not in the American fashion—the most disagreeable of all. We stopped at Auburn, celebrated for its prison; we dined there. But that is the painful side of travelling in America: it is impossible to eat the atrocious things they serve to you—tough meat, spiced, and stewed in the most awful sauces; impossible to get a cutlet, or even an egg.

LXXXIX.

ALBANY, September 8, 1841.

I HAVE been taking a walk through the city of Albany, which is situated on the Hudson and built in the shape of an amphitheatre; it has a grand appearance. When I get back to New York I shall have travelled sixteen hundred English miles, or four hundred French leagues, in nine days, sleeping every night in a hotel, except one night passed on Lake Ontario. The rapidity is wonderful, but very disagreeable on account of the bad management in the means of transportation and in the places one has to stop at.

XC.

NEW YORK, September 14, 1841.

A HORRIBLE affair has taken place here; General Alvear, the father of the victim, told me about it himself. On the 6th of the month, Mr. Alvear, a young man highly educated and with very agreeable manners, whose father is a

Member of Congress from one of the Southern States, was sitting with several young New-Yorkers in Niblo's Garden, when some one, who was known afterward to be a Mr. Suydam, struck him, from behind, three blows with a dagger, cutting his lips and horribly mutilating the lower part of his face. Niblo's Garden is the Tivoli of New York. Almost all the Americans carry daggers in their pockets. Mr. Alvear, taken by surprise, cried out, and tried to seize his assassin, who escaped without being interfered with by any of the spectators of this dreadful scene, and no policeman attempted to look for the murderer. Later one of Mr. Alvear's friends found Mr. Suydam, and asked him why he committed this cruel assault. He said, " Because Mr. Alvear made love to my wife." " But why did you not take your revenge like a man of honor?" Mr. Suydam replied, " I am not a man of honor in his eyes, but a *blackleg*, and he would not have fought with me." The newspapers gave an account of the affair, treating it in a jocose way, and laughing at Mr. Alvear for having written amorous letters to Mrs. Suydam. It seems that this lady has been known to have received favorably declarations more compromising than could be made by letter, and that Mr. Suydam was only a contraband husband and gambler by profession. What made it harder for Mr. Alvear to have received this attack from the husband was that one of his friends was the real culprit. In any case it is disgusting, and covers the American with a varnish of barbarism difficult to be found even amongst savages.

I hear that affairs in Washington are getting very much embroiled. President Tyler has vetoed a new bill; this is a very strong measure, and I think a wise one. All the members of his Cabinet resigned except Mr. Webster. The President immediately nominated others to replace them. Congress adjourned two days ago, but unfortunately before adjourning passed the famous bill which has given me so much care and trouble during the last six months. I am beaten, badly beaten, as I foresaw, and I expect a great outcry in France; but I feel that I have done all that I possibly could, and my mind is easy. The most scandalous scenes have taken place in Congress: insults passed, and even blows. What a curious world, or rather what a world of curious people!

To put a stop to things, a committee *ad hoc* was appointed: they proposed to fine any member one hundred dollars who should insult another, and to expel any one who should strike a blow. What manners! My God! what have I done to be obliged to live amongst such people? He who struck the first blow was one of those who were most useful to me in my difficulties about the duties. With all my heart I shall welcome my recall, should it be to transfer me to the Republic of San Marino. Everything about the Americans is repugnant to me—their opinions, their manners, their habits, their character! M. de Talleyrand often said that there was no base to American society, because moral sense did not exist in it. I am more and more impressed with the truth of this observation. Another social condition is wanting to the Americans, and that is the ties of family, which their anxiety for continual movement has succeeded in destroying. All the men are occupied in trying to make money, and only live for that: in their eyes a swindler is a very clever man, so long as he keeps within the law.

Mgr. Forbin-Janson has left here after having quarrelled with everybody: his church is hardly above ground; let anybody finish it who wants to.

XCI.

NEW YORK, September 17, 1841.

COMING back from my walk I met a long procession of Freemasons, who here take as much care to display their ribbons and emblems as their brothers in Europe do to conceal theirs. More than six hundred well-dressed men composed this procession. Freemasonry exists in the United States on a great scale; it is almost a political institution, and serves at the same time as a distraction to men who have so little to amuse them, and also of distinction to these fiery Democrats who, in spite of their pretended love of equality, strive to appear superior the one to the other.

Mr. Radgers, a banker who has large transactions with France, showed me everything connected with the two principal institutions in New York—the Custom-house and the Stock Exchange: this last edifice is built entirely of granite and iron.

XCII.

NEW YORK, September 20, 1841.

A STEAMER which touched at Halifax brings the news that the Prince de Joinville left that place for New York on the 16th; we expect him at any moment.

XCIII.

NEW YORK, September 21, 1841.

THE Prince de Joinville, for whom we have waited so long, was last night in sight of port, and will no doubt be here in a few hours. He sent the brig Cassard in advance.

The commander of the brig came to the French Consulate to get some packages which had been sent from Paris for the Prince, who, it seems, intends to spend six weeks in the

United States. After resting in New York four or five days, he will leave the Belle-Poule and the Cassard there, and travel through the interior of the United States.

XCIV.

NEW YORK, September 22, 1841.

OUR young Prince arrived yesterday: we had sent a steamboat to tow his vessel up, as there was no wind. M. de la Forest and I went on another steamboat to wait for him at Quarantine, where we supposed he would be detained. Just as we arrived he passed with his beautiful frigate, and pursued his way without being interfered with. We were obliged to retrace our steps, and arrived at New York shortly after him. We went on board the Belle-Poule, where the Prince received us in the most charming manner and kept us to dinner. It was four o'clock, and we were to dine at five; in the interval the Prince took me apart, and told me that the first time he came to the United States while in Washington he had behaved in such a way that he had now been sent back from France to make amends for his error. Mr. Van Buren, who was President at that time, asked him how long he intended to stay in Washington; he told him that he was going to leave next day. Notwithstanding this reply Mr. Van Buren invited him to dine next day, which invitation the Prince did not think he was obliged to accept. This produced great dissatisfaction and disagreeable remarks, which were reported on the other side of the Atlantic. The Prince charged M. Pontois to make his excuses, but he received a *fameux galop*,*—this is his expression,—and the King peremptorily ordered him to return to the United States and accept an invitation to dinner. Consequently he will go immediately to Washington and stay there long enough to avoid another scolding.

After that he will go to Norfolk to see the French vessels which are there, and then travel through the interior, visiting the Ohio, the Mississippi, etc., etc.

He told me all this in a very gay and lively

---

* Severe reprimand.

manner, treating me with great amiability. Positively he is a *charming prince*. His band, which is a very fine one, played during dinner, and I was delighted to hear French airs again. His frigate is a magnificent vessel, and I felt a profound joy mixed with sadness, feeling myself *in France* and surrounded by sailors speaking French. Unhappily I was sicker than usual. His Royal Majesty saw it, and ordered his physician to visit me this morning, and I am now waiting to see Doctor Guillard.

XCV.

New York, September 24, 1841.

I was at M. de la Forest's this morning when the Prince arrived there; he gave us his orders for the reception of the Consuls and all the French on board the Belle-Poule this morning.

I presented my attaché, M. de Montholon, to him, whom he was pleased to accept as his travelling companion in his journey through the interior. We made out a plan for his guidance, but I am afraid the season is so far advanced that he will be obliged to shorten this excursion. I am more and more ravished with our young Prince, who joins to a great dignity the most complete simplicity; he charms every one who has the honor to approach him.

I told him that Mr. and Mrs. Rivers had expressed a wish to pay their respects to him on board his frigate (Mr. Rivers was American Minister in Paris in 1830): he chose to go himself to see Mrs. Rivers, who was beside herself with joy, and of whom a great many were envious on account of this visit.

XCVI.

WASHINGTON, September 28, 1841.

I LEFT New York on the 25th, to precede the Prince, who arrives to-morrow; but I was disagreeably detained in Philadelphia by the puritanical hypocrisy which does not allow travelling on Sunday. I was, however, very anxious to be in Washington to prepare for the reception of his Royal Highness. I arranged this morning with Mr. Fox, the *doyen* of the Diplomatic Corps, the question of the visit which this Corps ought to pay him. I have also been to see the President, already notified of the arrival of the Prince, and who, after the information I caused to be transmitted to him from New York, was prepared to receive him. He was very anxious and desirous to be agreeable to his Royal Highness. Mr. Webster, Secretary of State, left Washington this morning. I am not sorry for this discourteous act, for he is pretentious, tiring, and would have bored us. Mr. Legare, one of the new Members of the Cabinet, who is amiable, and speaks French very well, will replace Mr. Webster, which will be far more agreeable for the Prince.

I must tell you of a charming piece of simplicity on the part of Miss Tyler, the daughter of the President, who by the way is very pretty. I had scarcely said good-evening yesterday, than she asked with a very injured air, "Is it true, sir, that the Prince of Joinville is engaged to a Princess of the Netherlands?" I hastened to assure her that my Prince, a very handsome young man, was absolutely free, and that all the American ladies could have a chance to gain his affections—

but I did not say his hand. I have no doubt that the idea of making herself agreeable to the Prince and marrying him was the thought in this young lady's mind.

XCVII.

WASHINGTON, September 30, 1841.

His Royal Highness arrived yesterday at eleven o'clock in the morning, with five officers: Captain Lugeol, commanding the brig Cassard; M. Touchard, aide-de-camp; M. Fabre, lieutenant of the Belle-Poule; M. Gervais, midshipman of the first class; and M. Roussin, son of the Admiral, midshipman of the second class.

I waited for the Prince at the railway station, and took him in my carriage to the hotel, where apartments had been kept for him; I told him of the arrangements made for his stay here, which, to his great satisfaction, need not be more than thirty-six hours.

I accompanied him to the President's, where the officers and the members of the Legation also were. The reception was rather dull. The

Prince told me that he was deafer than usual: he speaks very low, and is very timid about speaking English; the President could hardly hear him, much less understand him. His Royal Highness and all of us dine soon with Mr. Tyler.

The Prince, with his suite and all the Legation, dined with me yesterday; he appeared to enjoy a few hours' relief from public notice. He talked with great ease and good-humor. He is really endowed with remarkable intelligence, which he shows in everything he says without the slightest effort. He frankly told me that the future looked very threatening, and that a rupture between England and the United States was imminent. He placed the frigate and brig under my orders during his absence, leaving instructions to his officers to be guided by my advice.

XCVIII.

WASHINGTON, October 1, 1841.

THE Prince has just left for Baltimore. He told me that he was very well satisfied with his stay here, and with what I had done to make it as endurable and short as possible. I presented the Diplomatic Corps to him yesterday. Nothing particular occurred, except that Lord Prudhoe, brother of the Duke of Northumberland, and another Englishman, whose name I have forgotten, who had asked to be presented to his Royal Highness, came in frock-coats, and altogether badly dressed, which was more like the American than the English usage. They went to dinner at the President's later in dress-coats.

This dinner passed off better than I had hoped. It only lasted one hour and a half. Miss Tyler, with her usual simplicity and frankness, declared that she had *lost her heart* to my Prince, to whom I repeated this significant speech. Wishing to acknowledge it, he made up his mind to talk with Miss Tyler, although he had told me that his timidity was so great that he never talked with women.

The grand reception in the evening was ridiculous and tiresome. Happily the Prince with his natural gayety, amused himself with the strange toilettes of the women, and bore with great patience the indiscretion of all those who asked to be presented, also the familiarity of their manners and language. At last, at ten o'clock, he went home delighted to have performed the task for which he had crossed the ocean by royal and paternal command.

I shall have the honor to see the Prince again in New York, where he returns in three or four weeks to rejoin the Belle-Poule.

XCIX.

PHILADELPHIA, October 12, 1841.

I AM here on my way to New York. I have made a great many visits to-day. The city is in a state of excitement on account of the elections which are going on now. They are in favor of the Democratic Party, which is Mr. Van Buren's party, beaten last year.

I have been again to the house M. de Talleyrand lived in while in Philadelphia; it is on

North Third Street, facing the City Hotel. Fifty years ago it was the fashionable quarter, and now it is all shops. The ground-floor was occupied by a baker named Brescht, who is still alive, but does not live there now. I cannot look at this house without emotion.

I am writing to you with an accompaniment of inhuman cries and ferocious yells of the mob, who show their interest in the election in this way.

C.

NEW YORK, October 17, 1841.

M. DE LA FOREST took me to see two ladies who had very kindly expressed a wish to make my acquaintance—Mrs. B—— and Mrs. M——. The first is a daughter of General Reubel, who came to this country and was married at the same time as Jerome Bonaparte. Mrs. B—— is a rich widow, agreeable, and very pretty. She is bored here, and wishes to return to France, where she had amused herself very much. Mrs. M—— is the wife of a doctor. She has also lived a long time in France, where her husband went for his health, and they were both presented at Court by General Cape. The Prince of Joinville, who had seen them there, spent two evenings with Mrs. M—— very agreeably. This created quite a sensation in the city, and will make the family very *fashionable.* Mrs. M—— proposes to give a ball to the Prince on his return.

I went with the Baron de Marschall yesterday to see the packet-ship on which he embarks to-morrow for Europe. Happy mortal!

I also went to see Captain Charner, who is in command of the Belle-Poule in the absence of the Prince. I visited the ship throughout, and admired it very much. There appeared to me to be a falling-off in one thing—that is, in the discipline of the ship. I think the Prince allows too much liberty to his officers, probably fearing to appear more exacting than an ordinary commander. Their discipline suffers from it.

I dined yesterday with Mr. and Mrs. Mortimer Livingston. Their house is charming: it is the only one I have seen in the United States that is in really good taste and elegant.

They have eighty thousand francs a year, and
belong to one of the highest families in America. Mr. Livingston is as well-bred and polished as if he were not an American. His wife
is not pretty, but she tries to please, and succeeds. They have travelled, and know how
to converse. Mrs. B——, an intimate friend
of Mrs. Livingston, was the only woman at
this dinner. These ladies retired at dessert,
and we joined them an hour afterward in the
drawing-room.

I have just finished Messieurs de Tocqueville and de Beaumont's work on the Penitentiary System in the United States—a book
which has had great success in Europe, and
obtained the "Monthyon Prize." I think of
this book as I do of M. de Tocqueville's "Democracy" and the writings of Michel Chevalier—that they are interesting, but not accurate. Everything is arranged by the authors
to please a certain class of European readers.
These gentlemen commit a thousand errors in
their assertions, and pronounce opinions about
things they have never seen, or seen with a
fixed intention to make them serve to injure
our institutions, our French administration,

and to make for themselves a cheap popularity.

CI.

New York, October 22, 1841.

Mr. Coppinger, a rich merchant of New York, and Frenchman by birth, came to see me this morning, with an album belonging to a *young miss* under his arm. He brought it with a request from her—although I had never seen her—to put my name at the bottom of a list of American autographs. I refused, as politely as I could, to make myself ridiculous by figuring there. In looking over the album I saw a curious inscription. You know that after the affair at Strasbourg, Louis-Bonaparte went to Brazil, then to New York, from which place he returned to Europe. While he was here the lady of the album begged him to put his name in it. He thought fit to write a famous verse with his signature, which according to him depicted his position, and here is the quotation as written in the album:

"Le premier qui fut roi, fut un soldat heureux ;
Qui sert bien son pays n'a pas besoin d'aïeux !—(Racine.)
"Louis-Napoleon Bonaparte.
"New York, June 10, 1837."

What do you think of a French Prince who gives to Racine what belongs to Voltaire?

The name of the owner of the album is Miss Ward, daughter of a General of militia, and member of Congress. I know neither father nor daughter.

The French who are living here annoy me very much. My predecessor, M. Pontois, lived on very familiar terms with them, and they are astonished that I do not follow his example. Some of them expect me to pay the first visit, and invite me to their dinners and their parties without even leaving a card at my door. They are, taking them altogether, not very commendable. Misfortunes in business have brought most of them to the United States, where they seek and find fortunes. Therefore I have no desire to see more of them than is strictly necessary, and I have announced that I will return visits which are made to me, but that I will not pay a first visit to any one, and that I will accept invitations only from those who have sought to make my acquaintance.

CII.

New York, November 1, 1841.

I HAVE been to see Mrs. M—— again. She is an amiable woman, large, and very much like an English housekeeper. Her daughter, Miss Louisa, is not as pretty as Monseigneur the Prince of Joinville represented her to be. Mrs. M—— showed me the preparations for the ball she offered to the Prince on his return, and which he has accepted.

An unfortunate event has taken place here. The Catholic Bishop of New York is old, infirm, and childish; they have given him a coadjutor, Mr. Hughes, made on this account Bishop *in partibus* of Barianopolis. Mr. Hughes, who is an Irishman by birth, is very hot-headed and full of imprudent zeal, which has caused him to commit a fault very injurious to the interests of Catholicism in this country. Every year the Legislature of New York votes the funds to be distributed amongst the primary schools, all directed by Protestants. The Catholics have protested against this exclusive measure, and demanded part of these funds for schools founded by them. This protest has been taken into consideration and sustained by many influential persons, who recognize that as the Catholics pay their share of the taxes by the aid of which the schools are kept up, it is only just that they should have their share in the distribution. Bishop Hughes has insisted in the religious assemblies that justice should be done. If he had kept to this, nothing could have been better, and he would before long have obtained what he asked; but this is what he took into his head to do: the general election for one third of the Legislature being near at hand, he called a meeting more political than religious, where he gave an incendiary discourse, in which, not confining himself to generalities, he designated twelve candidates favorable to the distribution of funds to the Catholics. He so inflamed his audience, most of them poor Irish workmen, that in their excitement they behaved in a manner very much to be regretted. The next day the newspapers threw fire and flames against the Bishop, whom they accused of stirring up civil war. The twelve candidates designated by this violent prelate protested, and if they are elected, it is probable they will vote against the Catholics; besides, these senseless agitations of the clergy do a great deal of harm.

CIII.

NEW YORK, November 3, 1841.

WE had news of our young Prince yesterday, who, as I foresaw, has been delayed in his journey. The weather has been terrible: snow, excessive cold, and not sufficient water in the lakes to permit the steamboats to make their regular trips. Happily their gay party are well. M. Montholon writes me from Saint Louis that they hope to be in New York about the 22d or 23d.

Doctor Guillard, physician of the Belle-Poule, accompanied the Prince on his voyage to Saint Helena. General Bertrand, as you know, was there at the same time. Talking one day over their reminiscences of the Empire, the General said to the doctor, who he found shared the common prejudice against M. de Talleyrand and believed that he had betrayed the Emperor, that this report was entirely false, and that the Emperor had been altogether to blame in all their reciprocal relations. As M. de Talleyrand was dead and the General had gone to Saint Helena to bring the remains of the Emperor home, he could have nothing to gain, and his testimony must have great weight.

CIV.

New York, November 20, 1841.

Our young Prince arrived yesterday in good health, content with his journey and anxious to get away again. However, he has resigned himself to accept an invitation to attend a ball at Boston; he could not refuse without hurting their feelings. He will go to Boston day after to-morrow, return Friday morning to a dinner given to him by the French people here on that day, and in the evening will go to Mrs. M——'s ball. Saturday he will dine with the municipality of New York, Sunday he will sail, and I shall return to Washington.

CV.

NEW YORK, November 22, 1841.

THE Prince de Joinville attended Mass yesterday, after which he had the goodness to come to see me. He conversed for an hour on different subjects with great ability; nothing escapes him, and he never forgets anything; at his age, and with his simple manners and gay disposition, he has already a personal value which predicts a brilliant future.

CVI.

NEW YORK, November 24, 1841.

I WENT on board the Belle-Poule yesterday about noon to pay my respects to the Prince. He kept me to assist him to receive Mrs. Livingston and Mrs. De Pau, who had come to pay a visit to his Royal Highness and see the vessel. I afterward accompanied the Prince to the steamboat which was to take him, twelve of his officers, and M. de Montholon to Boston; they will all return here the day after tomorrow.

CVII.

New York, November 26, 1841.

My young Prince has just arrived from Boston; he is delighted, and from what M. de Montholon tells me, everything must have passed off very well. I am the more pleased because I had particularly urged that this invitation should be accepted; the Prince was very much opposed to it, wishing to avoid this obligation.

This is our great day—the French dinner at five o'clock, and at nine Mrs. M——'s ball.

CVIII.

New York, November 27, 1841.

The entertainment given by the French took place in the hall of a grand hotel called the Astor House. It was decorated with tricolored flags, and the band from the Belle-Poule, which is excellent, played wonderfully well, although a little too loud. The toasts were generally stupid enough, and the manners of the company pretty bad. The Prince had on his left the president of the banquet, M. Chegaray, an infirm old man, who proposed the toasts, and on his right the Mayor of New York; I sat next to him; on the other side an Alderman. It was in this position I had to pass three hours. The Prince left at half-past eight, and came home with me before going to the ball. The street I lived in being unpaved, we were obliged to get in and out of our carriages in a pouring rain, and on sidewalks wet and muddy.

Mrs. M——'s house was very well arranged and filled with the *fashion* of New York. This entertainment was a great event, and caused much gossip and many jokes. Poor Mrs. M—— will make many enemies and be much laughed at; they say she will be obliged to leave New York! This is her reward for having taken so much trouble. After examining the rooms and those who filled them, I came to the conclusion that although better than in Washington, there was much to find fault with in the exaggerated dress of the women and the vulgar manners of the men. I went home at eleven o'clock, the Prince having kindly advised me to take some rest.

CIX.

NEW YORK, November 28, 1841.

I ATTENDED his Royal Highness to the Corporation dinner. We arrived at six o'clock; they did not sit down to table until seven, and the dinner, which was a very bad one, ended at ten. The room was infected by gas and tobacco-smoke. The toasts, which were given by the Mayor, commenced at dessert, and were most flattering to the Prince and to France. The Mayor was seated on the right of his Royal Highness, and I on the left. Lord Morpeth, who happened to be in New York and was invited, was next to the Mayor. After all the official toasts were given—not very complimentary to England on account of the events they recalled—the health of Lord Morpeth was proposed. In returning thanks he took occasion to retaliate by some sharp and witty allusions to those toasts which had been disagreeable to him as an Englishman. His speech was a great success; but the true, the great, and sincere success rests with our Prince, who during his stay here has shown admirable tact, good taste, and cleverness.

After dinner we went to an impromptu dance, given by Mrs. Livingston, who had proposed it to the Prince at Mrs. M——'s last night. He danced and chatted with Miss M—— until two o'clock, when we escorted him to the wharf, and bade him farewell, as he was to sail at five o'clock this morning.

He said all sorts of kind things to me, and ordered me to visit him in Paris, where he hoped we should soon meet. He sent by M. de Montholon a very handsome bracelet to his wife, and left presents for three or four persons and alms for the poor.

CX.

PHILADELPHIA, November 30, 1841.

I AM fated to meet Fanny Elssler at Philadelphia; this is the fourth time. We live in the same hotel, and I have just been to see her. She says she is here on business, but that Mr. Wickoff—her friend she calls him, her lover some say, others again say he is her husband—has fallen ill, and she is waiting until he gets well to finish her engagement in New York.

She will not return to Europe this year; she expects her sister Thérèse, with whom she will spend the winter in Havana and New Orleans. She wants to go afterward to England and Germany, for she does not dare to enter France, where she has been condemned to pay sixty thousand francs to the Paris Opera. This is all this amiable girl had to tell. I found her changed, and pale. She had a severe illness in Boston.

CXI.

WASHINGTON, December 3, 1841.

HERE I am again in my prison, which seems to me more gloomy and horrible than ever. I am perishing with cold, in spite of the Franklin stoves and the Buffalo skins that I have nailed on the walls. I have not been consoled by a visit I made to Mr. Webster, who is just as *pompous* in his manners and English at heart as ever. I have also been to see the President, to thank him again, on the part of the Prince, for his kindness; but conversation with this good man, who is not very brilliant, is dull and fatiguing. His daughter, Miss Tyler, is more pretentious and ridiculous than ever since her head has been turned by dreams of grandeur.

CXII.

WASHINGTON, December 22, 1841.

EVERYBODY in Washington is very much concerned about a robbery of the Patent Office, which is about one hundred yards from my house. All the curiosities belonging to the Government are deposited in one of the rooms of this establishment, among others the snuff-boxes and other presents made to diplomatic agents of the United States, which they are forbidden by law to accept for themselves. The robbers got into this room in full light of day, and carried off everything; they have not been caught, and probably never will be, owing to the singular organization of the police, or rather the total absence of any guarantee of public or private property.

CXIII.

WASHINGTON, January 13, 1842.

I WENT to Congress to-day expecting to hear a speech from Mr. Clay, which has been much talked of, but it appears has been put off indefinitely. This is the great Mr. Clay who caused the election of poor General Harrison to the Presidency eighteen months ago, after exacting from him the assurance that he would not be a candidate again at the end of his four years' term, hoping to succeed him; but Mr. Tyler having succeeded after only a month's occupancy by the poor General, and having also boldly vetoed a law proposed by Mr. Clay, and by which he (Clay) hoped to increase his popularity, has made for himself a declared enemy. Thus the great Clay thinks only of revenging himself on the present President: he intends proposing to Congress to alter the Constitution so that the power of the President may be more restricted, and the length of his term of office diminished; that his veto shall be suspensive, and not definite; that the Secretary of the Treasury shall be elected by

Congress, which would make him independent of the President. All these revolutionary propositions, tending to weaken the power of the President, are dictated by a desire for revenge: if they were adopted they would destroy the harmony and the balance of power which, in the opinion of the authors of the Constitution, ought to guarantee the maintenance and the tranquillity of the country. Behold the patriotism and civil virtue of the great American citizens!—they think of procuring for themselves authority, power, and office, just as the great men in our constitutional monarchies seek to obtain all that; but the one takes it and the other asks for it—that is all the difference.

As to the result of Democratic institutions on the finance of the country, here is an instance: eight years ago the United States paid every cent of their National debt, and the fact was proclaimed throughout Europe as being wonderful, and as a substantial proof of the merit of their form of government; now, eight years after, the United States have contracted a new debt of twelve hundred million francs. Five of the States declare they will not pay this debt. The Bank of Philadelphia has failed to the amount of fifty million francs, and five hundred banks in other parts of the country are insolvent. All the public works, so much talked about, have been built with money borrowed from Europe, which they refuse to repay; the result is that most of these enterprises which have been undertaken remain unfinished. As to the Federal Government, whose seat is in Washington, there is a deficit of seventy thousand francs for the year 1842. They find it impossible to borrow at six per cent, and are obliged to give seven and eight. During these eight years in which these disasters have occurred there has been no extraordinary expenditure; the army is only ten thousand men for a population of seventeen millions; the navy is so small that it cannot compete with any in Europe; the only extra expense has been a war in Florida against eight hundred Seminole Indians, whom they have not been able to subdue after eight years' struggle, and this war has cost one hundred and fifty million francs, owing to the shameful extravagance of those who have been employed to manage it. Now this is the situation of this great and beautiful country, which the revolutionists and imbeciles in France have so vaunted for their economical institutions and fraternal feelings. This financial result and the general condition, which offers no security, proves conclusively that democracy is incapable of governing.

I went yesterday at five o'clock to dine with the President: forty men; no women—they did not appear till after dinner. I was placed between Mr. Spencer and Mr. Webster; the latter forgot his contraband dignity with which he usually conceals his sad mediocrity. The Madeira wine, of which he drank entirely too much, made him not only amiable, I mean in the American sense, but most tenderly affectionate; he took my arms with both hands, and said, "My dear Bacourt, I am so glad to see you to-night—more so than I have felt at any other time: I do not know why! Perhaps I have not been as friendly with you as I ought to have been, but if you are willing we will become bosom friends. You will find me a good companion; come and see me every day without ceremony; it will give me great pleasure, my dear Bacourt, for, really, I think you are charming." This flattering declaration was made with a drunken stammer, and —shall I dare to say it—with hiccups, which made it very disagreeable to be near this Minister of Foreign Affairs. And this occurred at the table of the President of the United States, at a dinner given to the representatives of all the European powers!

CXIV.

WASHINGTON, January 25, 1842.

I HAVE heard Mr. Clay's famous speech, which has been talked of as the great event for the last three weeks; but it was not a success—a complete failure! Lord Morpeth was there, and had an opportunity of judging of the eloquence of the great American orators, and of the anarchy which rules in this paradise called a republic! The scenes in Congress are every day more disgusting. After a session of seven weeks, they have not agreed upon anything. In the Hall of Representatives they have insulted each other in the grossest manner, and outside they have fought with their fists; it is an unheard-of and revolting spectacle.

CXV.

WASHINGTON, February 3, 1842.

OLD Mr. Adams raised a tremendous storm in Congress yesterday. This man, seventy-two years old, was President of the United States for four years, but not being elected for a second term, has been at enmity with the whole world ever since. After having occupied the highest position, he sought the secondary honor of representing his own State in Congress, and in that position has for several years agitated the whole country with the terrible question of abolition of slavery, which infuriates the representatives of the South, where slavery exists, where it is almost indestructible; and in any event, rumors of abolition can only excite the slaves against their masters, and might bring about a civil war. Notwithstanding these facts, Mr. Adams undertook, ten days ago, to bring before the House a petition which had been sent to him by some inhabitants of a little town in Massachusetts, asking the dissolution of the Union, urging as a pretext that the existence of slavery in the South will be the cause of permanent hostility between the North and the South. This is the first time that the great word Dissolution has been pronounced, as it were, officially in Congress, and it produced the greatest excitement. It was proposed to declare the petition an act of high treason, and that Mr. Adams deserved to be driven from the Hall for having presented it; but that in consideration of his age, and the position he had occupied in the country, the House, after having passed a vote of censure on him, left him to the remorse of his conscience. During eight sessions they have discussed these propositions with a grossness of language which no one could conceive who had not been present at these scandalous scenes, both degrading to the Government and the Nation. For my part, I am delighted at all this *mischief*, which injures Mr. Adams, the only man I have politically to find fault with in this country, and, besides, lowers still more these democratic institutions which America has disgusted me with.

Lord Morpeth spends his whole time in Congress. The members, so proud of having an English Lord amongst them, give him a seat on the floor of the House, and he appears to be *quite at home!*

CXVI.

WASHINGTON, February 4, 1842.

I MET yesterday a Mr. and a Mrs. Bayard, who have the impudence to call themselves descendants of the Chevalier Bayard; they were ignorant no doubt of the fact that he had the good sense never to marry. These ridiculous Americans have adopted arms with the device, "Sans peur et sans reproche!" Walking with M. de Montholon this morning, he pointed out to me two *misses* of sixteen or seventeen years old as the Misses Bayard, who were arm-in-arm with two young men. Some one observed to the mother lately that it was a singular liberty to allow young girls to go everywhere alone with young men, and talk in corners first with one and then another. The mother said that she did not think it was altogether proper, but that it was out of the power of parents to prevent it unless young girls were kept shut up and deprived entirely of the companionship of persons of their own age, and that if this was done they would rebel, and become independent and unmanageable. Eight girls out of nine marry against the wishes of their parents here, and elopements are frequent from Protestant schools: so much so that the Catholic schools, where the management is so much better, are preferred even by Protestant parents.

CXVII.

WASHINGTON, February 15, 1842.

I HAVE been to see Mrs. Kennedy and Mrs. Winthrop. Their husbands are members of the House of Representatives, and on the committee having charge of commercial affairs, in which I am interested. They are the most distinguished men amongst this strange American people. The Kennedys are from Baltimore and the Winthrops from Massachusetts, of which one of his ancestors was Governor two hundred years ago.

They say that these gentlemen are very particular about visits from foreign Ministers to their wives. I have also been to see the Secretary of the Treasury about commercial affairs, with which I am constantly occupied. Congress seems at last disposed to discuss this question. I have taken great pains about it; but so far everything has been against me. The great need of money by the United States Government has forced them to increase the duties on all foreign productions. However, I am satisfied with my interview with the Secretary of the Treasury.

CXVIII.

WASHINGTON, February 17, 1842.

WASHINGTON IRVING has been appointed Minister to Spain: he is a man of intelligence and polished manners.

Charles Dickens, a great literary celebrity, is here; he is very popular both in England and in the United States, where his democratic writings secure him a brilliant reception. Entertainments are offered to him in every town he goes through; at New York they gave him a ball, attended by five thousand persons, where they had living tableaux of the principal scenes in his novels. It is a species of madness amongst the Americans, who always go to extremes in everything. The newspapers admit that he is made more of than Lafayette, Fanny Elssler, or the Prince of Joinville: this is the order the newspaper from which I quote places them in.

M. Mathews, the Catholic curé, tells me that President Tyler's sister, who is a Catholic, lives in Washington and keeps a *boardinghouse*, that is to say, a *pension bourgeois*—a very common resource here for poor widows. The President has so much respect for the Catholics that it is reported he will join their religion. I do not believe it.

I received a letter from our Consul in Philadelphia; it describes the situation in Pennsylvania so well that I copy it for you. You must know that scarcely six years ago Philadelphia was in the most prosperous condition.

"We are in the most alarming situation:

confidence is entirely destroyed; our Legislators, who are ignorant and corrupt, will do nothing to extricate their unfortunate constituents from the abyss of misery and ignominy in which they are sunk; those from whom we claim what is due to us laugh in our faces, saying, 'When we are paid by those who owe us we will pay you.' But when they have bank-notes which they are anxious to get rid of, they pay you in advance, and if an hour after having received these notes you could not pass, you take them back, they coolly say, 'Well, you ought not to have taken them!' Besides, they say that this is the last time that Pennsylvania will pay the interest on her debt. Most of these State bonds are owned abroad, which gives greater force to this doctrine of repudiation—a doctrine very popular here, consisting of not paying their debts. I advise my French compatriots to send to France all they can realize at any sacrifice. All the banks are ruined; the populace want to reduce every one who has any wealth to their own level. If the affairs of the Union are not better managed than those of the States; if ignorance, party spirit, cupidity, and egotism should prevent Congress adopting suitable measures; and if the bad faith of the people of this country brings on a foreign war—what will become of us?"

This is the picture of a country whose organization has been lauded to the sky; and, for having proclaimed it sublime M. de Tocqueville has been made member of all the academies, and Michel Chevalier overwhelmed with honors.

CXIX.

WASHINGTON, April 1, 1842.

THE last news from Europe has caused great excitement here: the declaration of Lord Aberdeen, indorsed by seven peers who are the best authorities on international law, that the negroes found on board the Creole ought not to be restored to the United States, is considered by many people and by almost all the newspapers as equivalent to a declaration of war.

The debates in the French Chamber of Deputies on the right of search, and their refusal to ratify the treaty of December 20, signed by the five great Powers to which our Government has been obliged to submit, has also produced a great sensation. These new events will make Lord Ashburton's mission here much more difficult; he is expected every day.

News has been received that hostilities have commenced between the republics of Mexico and Texas, which has also caused great excitement in Washington. This last is a regular nest of bandits from everywhere, but particularly from the United States. When they speak of a robber, an assassin or a bankrupt, they say he has left his cards—G. T. T. (gone to Texas), as we put P. P. C. Well, this honorable republic, which France, thanks to the advice of my predecessor, M. Pontois, was the first to acknowledge, is about to declare war against Mexico.

I have been to hear Mr. Clay's farewell address to the Senate; he is going to retire, after thirty-six years of service in it. It was an occasion on which to make a great speech, but in my opinion his was *quite a failure:* he tried to be touching, and pretended to cry in the most ridiculous manner. It was the silly talk of a worn-out old man—nothing more. His partisans also thought themselves obliged to weep, while his opponents laughed in the most impudent manner. I went to see him next day: he affected to be in a very happy and contented state of mind, wanted to play at the rat retiring in his cheese, but very plainly let it be seen that he had not renounced the hope of being elected President in three years.

CXX.

WASHINGTON, April 18, 1842.

YOU can have no idea of the trouble the least thing here gives you; money will not always procure you the simplest things: for a box that I wanted to send to France, I was obliged to go first to a carpenter to order the box, then to a sail-maker for linen to cover it with, from there to another man to tar it, and to a fourth to have it packed. I lost my patience and my temper at the air of condescension of these men to their customers. If you send your order by a servant, they pay not the slightest attention to it.

I was delighted to meet Lord Ashburton again: he has arrived at last, after a long and disagreeable passage. He recalled to me what M. de Talleyrand had said in speaking of the United States fifty years ago, "It is a giant in his cradle." He could say now that the giant had passed from his cradle into decrepitude.

There has been a riot in New York on the occasion of the municipal elections; in this riot they sacked Bishop Hughes's house, to punish him for having taken such an active part in political questions; but he is only Coadjutor, and the Incumbent, Mgr. Dubois, who is eighty-three years old, was not at all respected by the mob, notwithstanding his great age and infirmities. The authorities arrived two hours after the pillage.

A frightful accident took place at Baltimore the day before yesterday. On a trial-trip of a new steamboat with one hundred passengers the boiler burst, and more than three fourths were killed or mutilated! *So much for the American prudence.*

The tariff question is going very badly:

the want of money in the treasury is so great, that they will put higher duties than last year on foreign merchandise; French silks and wines suffer very much; but if things go as they say they will, the products of France will be treated better than any others. But it is fated that I shall meet with nothing but misfortunes in this country. The last post from New York has brought me more disagreeable news: the French who are engaged in business in New York are generally abominable rogues who have run away from France and live here by fraud. They have conspired against me on account of a letter I wrote lately to one of the worst of them, and have held a meeting for the purpose of formulating a complaint against me, which they intend to send to the Chamber of Deputies, accusing me of refusing them aid and protection. And yet everybody says that not one of my predecessors ever took more trouble than I have done about the private interests of the French in the United States. I shall be obliged to disclose their baseness to my Government. I have fallen here into a veritable hedge of thorns.

CXXI.

WASHINGTON, June 9, 1842.

IN three days eleven fires in Washington! As most of the houses were isolated and uninhabited, and no fires have been made in them during the winter, this must have been the work of incendiaries.

The President of the Committee on Ways and Means of the House of Representatives, of whom I had asked a few moments' interview, much to my surprise appointed this meeting at eight o'clock in the morning. I was there punctually, but to my greater astonishment as I thought I should find him alone, he was surrounded by nine members of his committee, not one of whom I knew, and I was obliged to discuss with these nine fellows the most delicate questions relating to my mission. I was examined and cross-examined. I am ignorant of what impression I made upon these individuals, but assuredly they did not impress me as gentlemen.

We have had such cold weather that we have been obliged to have fires everywhere, and that in the middle of June, in a country situated in the same latitude with Naples and Lisbon. But perhaps this excessive cold will keep off yellow-fever, which has made its appearance in New York. M. de la Fosse has returned from Havana and Saint-Domingo; his accounts of them are very interesting, and are worth the trouble I have to take to draw them out of him, for with great intelligence, he is very reticent, and dislikes talking. I cannot make out whether it is laziness or want of confidence in himself; if any State secrets are betrayed nobody should accuse him. At the same time he has the gift of observation, and has related things about the sentiments, religious practices, and manners and customs of these black people which pass belief. It is a republic of monkeys, nothing more. M. de la Fosse escaped by a miracle from the last earthquake, which destroyed fifteen thousand people at Saint-Domingo.

I saw at the President's house the portrait of M. Guizot, by Healy, an American painter who lived in Paris, and a copy of a portrait of General Washington which he made for our King. M. Guizot having written an introduction to the works of General Washington, which works he had translated, the Americans residing in Paris wished to have his portrait. They had him painted by Healy, and sent it to the President to place wherever he thought fit: he has given it to the National Institute of Sciences. Our King paid Mr. Healy five thousand francs to return to his country and copy the portrait of General Washington: this was independent of the price of the copy, which he had not much trouble in making better than the detestable original. Guizot's portrait appears to me to be very good: unfortunately he is standing, which shows the small stature of this great Minister, deputy, and orator.

The King's generosity to Mr. Healy has had a good effect here. The newspapers have been very liberal with the *flourish* on this occasion.

CXXII.

WASHINGTON, June 30, 1842.

I WENT to see the President, to give him a letter from the King; instead of receiving me in the drawing-room as usual, I was shown upstairs into a room where the whole Cabinet were assembled. This reception appeared to me, and in fact was, very strange—even in a country where customs are so singular. I only stayed long enough to hand my Sovereign's letter to Mr. Tyler, and retired, wishing the President and his council a happy result from their deliberations. When I returned I said to M. de la Fosse that I had no doubt that something very serious was being prepared. Two hours afterward the House of Representatives received a message from the President announcing that he had put his veto on the Tariff Bill which had been submitted to him two days before. This species of *coup d'état* may have the most serious consequences. It makes a complete split between the President and the majority in Congress. Will civil war break out? It exists in the little State of Rhode Island already: the two armies are in presence of each other there; martial law has been proclaimed, and all that under the walls of a city named Providence—a name so suited to a civil war.

CXXIII.

WASHINGTON, July 6, 1842.

THE anniversary of the Declaration of Independence of the United States was celebrated on the Fourth of July with the usual noise and excitement, but without any disasters. The deplorable political and financial situation of the country must cause many to reflect on this independence which they have exulted in for the last seventy years; and I am convinced that more than one man has had sense enough to curse, if not the independence itself, at least the institutions which have been the consequence of it.

I have just read in the *Journal des Débats* the great debate on the right of search, in which *Maréchal* Sébastiani showed so plainly his stupid presumption. He tried to imitate M. de Talleyrand in signing Protocols without instructions. This debate on the Treaties of

1831, 1833, and 1834 have recalled circumstances which cause me once more to admire the great intelligence and foresight of M. de Talleyrand, who was always opposed to a reciprocal right of search between France and England. This was so well known, that in 1831 and 1833, when he signed so many treaties between France and England, those treaties made in Paris between Lord Granville and General Sébastiani were not proposed to him, but kept concealed from him—General Sébastiani wishing, no doubt, to show that it was not M. de Talleyrand—who accomplished everything at London. I can still recall the anger and rage of M. de Talleyrand when the Treaty of 1831 was communicated to him. His sound judgment enabled him to foresee the bad consequences of this treaty.

The situation here is getting more and more complicated. The President's veto has so enraged his enemies that they talk of impeaching him; but this is folly, and nothing serious can come from it.

Our silks are better treated than I expected; but in revenge our wines are threatened with great cruelty. Notwithstanding the full powers I have received from Paris, I cannot leave here until the treaty with Lord Ashburton has been signed and the vote been taken on the tariff.

Two more American boats have blown up—one on the Mississippi, where seventy-two persons have perished; the other on one of the northern lakes, where they have already found forty-five dead bodies; most of these victims in both places are German emigrants, who are flooding this country just now. There were more than one hundred thousand emigrants from Europe last year, and probably will be fifty thousand more this year.

They must be very unhappy in Europe!

I have just received a letter from Monseigneur Chauch, Bishop of Natchez. He asks me to beg the King to give him a picture and the Queen a clock for the cathedral he has built. I will forward his request, which no doubt will be received as usual very graciously.

CXXIV.

WASHINGTON, July 25, 1842.

THE treaty between Lord Ashburton and the United States has been concluded, which facilitates my departure. I hope to embark on the Great Western at New York on the 11th of August. I leave here on the 30th, and will breathe the purer air of New York for ten days before commencing my voyage. I shall thank Heaven when I feel that I have placed the ocean between me and this dreary abode.

I have made a long round of visits of adieu; everywhere they say, "What! you are going away? When do you return? What! you do not intend to return! It is too bad to leave us, and without taking an American wife." This last remark was repeated by every one I saw: it gives you an idea of American taste.

www.ingramcontent.com/pod-product-compliance
Lightning Source LLC
Chambersburg PA
CBHW032047230426
43672CB00009B/1503